How to Talk
to a
Borderline

How to Talk to a Borderline

Joan Lachkar

Routledge
Taylor & Francis Group
New York   London

Routledge
Taylor & Francis Group
270 Madison Avenue
New York, NY 10016

Routledge
Taylor & Francis Group
27 Church Road
Hove, East Sussex BN3 2FA

© 2011 by Taylor and Francis Group, LLC
Routledge is an imprint of Taylor & Francis Group, an Informa business

International Standard Book Number: 978-0-415-87649-0 (Hardback)

Library of Congress Cataloging-in-Publication Data

Lachkar, Joan.
    How to talk to a borderline / by Joan Lachkar.
       p. ; cm.
    Includes bibliographical references and index.
    Summary: "In How to Talk to a Borderline, Joan Lachkar introduces Borderline Personality Disorder (BPD) and outlines the challenges and difficulties it presents to clinicians. She expands current understanding of BPD by outlining eight different kinds of borderline personality disorders and how each of these requires specific communication techniques and methods. Case examples are offered throughout the text and in some cases describe the kinds of partners borderlines attract. This book offers new approaches to communicating, working with, and treating borderline personality disorders while integrating more contemporary treatment methods"--Provided by publisher.
    ISBN 978-0-415-87649-0 (hardback : alk. paper)
    1. Marital psychotherapy. 2. Borderline personality disorder--Patients--Family relationships. 3. Borderline personality disorder--Classification. I. Title.
    [DNLM: 1. Borderline Personality Disorder. 2. Communication. 3. Professional-Patient Relations. WM 190 L137h 2010]

RC488.5.L3474 2010
616.89'1562--dc22
                                                 2010021220

Visit the Taylor & Francis Web site at
http://www.taylorandfrancis.com

and the Routledge Web site at
http://www.routledgementalhealth.com

To my family

Contents

Acknowledgments

I would like to begin by acknowledging my colleagues and supervising analysts, who have shown deep empathy in my struggle to treat and interact with my borderline patients. Their guidance and knowledge has given me the strength and the courage to genuinely believe that these people are really not out to get me; rather, they are people living in pain and terror who come to treatment to learn how to survive in a world that misrepresents and misunderstands them.

Many of the same dedicated friends and colleagues have remained loyal and supportive as I continue on my publishing journey. Many thanks to Peter Berton, distinguished professor emeritus at the School of International Relations, University of Southern California, who was most instrumental in helping me understand the cross-cultural narcissist and borderline. I believe I have learned more about Japanese, Russian, and Chinese cultures and politics from him than if I had lived in those countries myself. Much appreciation to my good friend and colleague Dr. Nancy Kobrin, whose corresponding work on global terrorism and suicide bombers has added greatly to my understanding of borderline pathology, which shares many of the characteristics of "borderland" or borderline culture (as those now being deployed to Afghanistan are finding out). Special tribute to George Zimmar, my publisher, for his steady encouragement and expansive vision of psychoanalytic theory that extends to the artistic, political, and global arena, and to his editorial assistant, Marta Moldvai, as well as all those at Routledge/Taylor & Francis for their invaluable support and encouragement.

Much gratitude to many others for their inspirational help: my amazing editor, Joanne Freeman, for her remarkable editorial skills and quick eye, who with her magic pen has done wonders for this manuscript. Special thanks to Lloyd deMause for introducing me to psychohistory; his endless dedication to my work, bountiful knowledge, and ongoing influence have encouraged me to continue on the path of studying and defining conflict that moves far beyond the confines of the consultation room. Also to Jamie Glazov, editor of *Frontpage Magazine,* who embraced my work and allowed me to publish my insights on terrorism from a psychodynamic perspective.

I must also pay special tribute to the many mentors who helped guide me through the complex and intricate process of psychoanalysis: Drs. Irene Fruchtbaum, James Grotstein, Peter Loewenberg, Albert Mason, Martha Trowbridge, Marvin Osman, Robert Kahn, and Roberta Rinaldi (who helped revise the mental status exam), among others. The master theorists who have helped provide a strong clinical basis for this book include Drs. Otto Kernberg, Wilfred Bion, Melanie Klein, Heinz Kohut, Sam Vaknim, and many others quoted throughout this volume. I would also like to thank my research assistant Khathy Hoang, who with a flash of an eye was able to zip through this manuscript with lightning speed.

I am indebted to the following good friends and colleagues for their endless patience and amazing analytic ears: Dr. Shelley Ventura, Myrna Goodman, Laurence Rose, and also to Drs. Jacob Bardov, Shelley Ventura, and Orli Peter for their scrupulous critiquing and insightful, firsthand expertise on the Middle East. I am grateful to my family, particularly my daughters: Sharon Stone, Dr. Pamela Brody, and Nicole Raphael, for their encouragement, patience, and sacrifices. I owe special thanks to Dr. Brody, Senior Clinical Instructor of Psychiatry at the University of Colorado, who was the first to introduce me to Marsha Linehan's work on Dialectic Behavioral Therapy (DBT). In addition, I wish to express singular gratitude to the entire staff at the New Center for Psychoanalysis for their contin- ued support and efforts, with particular appreciation for the late Dr. Joan Schain, Dr. Samuel Eisenstein, and Alexander Rogawsky for their never- ending encouragement.

In addition to my friends and colleagues from the analytic world, there are those from the dance and artistic world of classical ballet. For years I kept these worlds apart, not knowing how to integrate them until I wrote an article on "Dance and Narcissism," published in the *Journal of Dance and Choreography.* I owe much to the editor Bonnie Ota, to dance masters Margaret Hills and Hamed Nadar, and to the late Carmelita Maracci and Stanley Holden. Finally, and most important, I must give a profound thank you to my students, supervisees, and patients for their trust and devotion. They have turned out to be my best supervisors and teachers.

Introduction

Living in Borderland

Seal up the mouth of outrage for a while 'til we can clear these ambiguities.

—William Shakespeare, *Taming of the Shrew*

Welcome to Borderland: a world that knows no bounds and breeds a uniquely complex and fascinating group of individuals with borderline personality disorder (BPD). Of all the disorders, borderlines are the most puzzling personality type—not only for the therapists who treat them but also for the partners, families, and others who live, love, and interact with them. As Marsha Linehan, a leading expert on BPD, notes, "Borderline individuals are the psychological equivalent of third-degree-burn patients. Lacking emotional skin, they feel agony at the slightest touch or movement" (1993a). Borderlines are completely vulnerable and live in constant pain. They simply do not have an emotional boundary to protect their inner psyche. People who live in Borderland (also referred to as "Borderville") make up their own rules, have a weak hold on reality, are unpredictable, impulsive, and volatile; and hear what they want to hear. The term *Borderland* is not meant to be pejorative in any way but to call attention to a most mysterious disorder that has baffled the clinicians and mental health professionals who treat it.

The following dream is reflective of a borderline patient desperately trying to get out of Borderland.

> I had a dream that I was in an old broken-down home, with weird people entering the room, all muttering nonsense, all stuck together with glue. I tried desperately to escape before they globbed onto me. I knew I had to run away to avoid getting glued to them.

Never before has the challenge of treating borderline personality disorder been so widely acknowledged by clinicians and the public at large. Throughout the United States, hospitals, clinics, and mental centers have been created to treat those with BPD (mainly following the innovative work of Marsha Linehan). Yet clinicians and others who interact with borderlines find it difficult to understand their baffling behavior and defenses and to choose the right words to maximize treatment and create real communication.

Some borderlines are lonely, deprived individuals with no identity, while others are cultlike types who join up with those who share their pathology (often those who share traumatic childhoods and have become split and disassociated) and offer the validation and confirmation that borderlines seek. In the most subtle and insidious manner, borderlines have a way of making others feel and suffer the pain and devastation they experience and cannot contain or tolerate (known in psychoanalytic terms as projective identification). The term "borderline" has universal application because it not only has clinical significance but has spread globally into the world of abuse, violence, and terrorism. Although not all borderlines are terrorists per se, we have heard the horror stories about men, for example, putting burning flames to their wives or gouging out their children's eyes. In essence, borderlines are very taxing on the therapist, especially those who struggle to maintain the therapeutic boundaries (Grotstein, 1993).

There has been a voluminous amount of material written and a flurry of research on the borderline personality (Lachkar, 1993b). This includes a plethora of material that addresses the theoretical aspects of the borderline, as well as the psychodynamics and defense mechanisms within the borderline spectrum. Yet, very little has been written about how to actually talk to a borderline. It seems obvious that learning specific communication styles to address patients with severe borderline personality pathology would be beneficial not only for the therapist but also for the patients treated. Of course, this learning inundates us with technical terms such as empathy, containment, mirroring, and attunement, as well as the need to address defense mechanisms such as splitting, projection, projective identification, magical thinking, paranoid anxiety, and distortion/delusions. These concepts certainly hold much clinical relevance. However, this book goes beyond clinical terms to specifically spell out how to communicate with a borderline, using the language most suited for and palatable to each type of borderline described in this book.

In order to bond with and understand the borderline, one must first learn and speak their particular language of distortions and misperceptions. Marsha Linehan's work with Dialectic Behavioral Therapy (DBT) offers many useful approaches (Frugetti, 2006; Linehan, 1993a, 1993b). One of her approaches urges the borderline to find something to agree upon rather than be argumentative. It becomes a movement between acceptance and change and how each enhances the other. Another focuses on "distress-tolerance skills," which deals with the ability to accept the patient's mental state in a nonevaluative and nonjudgmental fashion. This does not mean approval for bizarre behavior in a given situation, but reserving judgment as a way to begin observing how one's emotions impact another. Giving myself the poetic freedom to abstract Marsha Linehan's concept of "Dialectics," I have extended it to what I term "The Language of Dialectics," a concept I devised to apply to the various borderlines described in this book. This is parallel to the "Language of Empathology" I originated in my book *How to Talk to a Narcissist* (Lachkar, 2008b), which employed Kohut's innovative work on self-psychology and the importance of empathy (Kohut, 1971, 1977).

Although there are many different techniques and approaches to treating borderlines, many of us acknowledge that we are dealing with resistance to change. Linehan recites the example of a patient who refused to do anything in her workbook manual. While Linehan "accepted" the patient's resistance, she also realized that if the patient played by the book she would improve and no longer need the group. In more simplistic terms, we could call this the BPD's dilemma. One of my patients was more direct and exclaimed, "Well, if I improve, then I will have to leave you and go out into the 'real' world."

My approach addresses both sides of the split for the borderline, but leaves me a bit leery about "accepting" the patient's defenses. For example, if the patient threatens suicide, I might, on the one hand, acknowledge the "real threat" and check out any dangers of a suicide attempt. Then I would move into the analytic direction (addressing the split-off or disassociated part), delving into how the patient commits emotional suicide (killing off all needs, feelings, and ambition, paralysis, depression). Using the language of dialectics, we might address this threat as follows:

> *Yes, of course there can be a real suicide where you end your life, but there can also be emotional suicide, part of you that murders and kills off all healthy needs, feelings, and desire in you.*

Thus, it becomes a physical suicide versus a psychological suicide. This opens up a new space to the patient and detoxifies the terror, which enables the patient to think in a new way. The same would apply to the narcissist when discussing the importance of empathy. I stress how we need to empathize with the patient's vulnerability but not the aggression—for example, "I understand how you feel like beating your wife because she does things to enrage you, but you are not allowed to beat her."

This book is an expansion of my previously published work, with an entirely new focus. Over the years, my writings have focused primarily on narcissistic/borderline relationships, mainly on what happens when a narcissistic and a borderline join together in a marital bond, and the impact their behavior and psychodynamics have on one another—what I refer to as "the dance" (Lachkar, 1992, 2004b). In *The Narcissistic/Borderline Couple* (Lachkar, 2004b), I noted how one partner stirs up many painful, unresolved, vulnerable feelings in the other, and how the other partner internalizes and identifies with these feelings; how each pushes some vulnerable spot in the other—for example, the borderline's shame and the narcissist's guilt. This inspired me to write *The V-Spot* (Lachkar, 2008a), which will be described later in this text.

A very good friend and colleague familiar with my work encouraged me to go beyond the psychodynamics of narcissistic/borderline relations and write about how they can actually talk or communicate with one another. Simply stated, he suggested I write a book on *How to Talk to a Narcissist* (then he suggested I do same with *How to Talk to a Borderline,* employing the Language of Dialectics). At this point, I hesitated because I did not want to diminish a scholarly endeavor to the level of a series of books on "How to Talk to . . . for Dummies" but was reassured that the scholarly effort would not be diminished.

I also feared there would be too much carryover or repetition from my other books, especially since narcissist and borderline states, traits, and characteristics do tend to vacillate back and forth, particularly the grandiose self, which also pervades many other disorders. However, although they do have similar defenses as narcissists, borderlines are different characters, with different faces and focuses. Since the focal point is on communication, one way I found to "talk the talk" was to note the distinctive and qualitative differences in each type of borderline. My colleagues reassured me that there is enough uniqueness and difference to make this effort worthwhile. For example, both the narcissist and the borderline may want the same things, but the narcissist tries to get needs met through entitlement, whereas the borderline does this through attack, revenge, and victimization. Also, the way one speaks to an antisocial borderline with severe superego pathology—one who lacks conscious guilt or the capacity for remorse—is quite different from how one speaks to an obsessive–compulsive borderline who has a severe restrictive superego and harsh sense of guilt. Having said all this, sometimes it is best to communicate and at other times best to contain, hold, wait, or in some instances attempt no communication (minus Talk or –Talk).

Since writing about these disorders, I have been flooded by borderline patients sending me articles, books, references, and Web sites to help me figure them out, even reassuring me about the importance of writing about the borderline, especially since people are less familiar with the borderline personality than with the narcissist. Everyone knows about narcissism and many claim this persona has held center stage too long.

My work in psychohistory and social science has given me insights into the chapter on the cross-cultural borderline (Lachkar, 1992, 2004b, 2008a, 2008b). It was astonishing to see how numerous tyrannical leaders and terrorists in the Middle East share many of the same dynamics that fall within the scope of BPD. In many of my publications, I refer to these leaders as malignant narcissists and borderlines. Terrorism has become one of the most frightening threats of our time. Most people agree it is not a simple task to negotiate or communicate with a terrorist; it is helpful to know what kind of terrorist we are talking about, e.g., an antisocial terrorist with a conscience, or a terrorist without a conscience (it may be a sadistic superego but it is still a conscience). Although most of the people we treat are not married to terrorists, many are married to a malignant borderline: someone who is abusive, cruel, and sadistic. Thus, the spouse may experience the same kind of emotional/physical pain as women in the Middle East whose human rights violations lead to devastating effects of oppression. This book's chapter on the Cross-Cultural Borderline details how people from different cultures bring with them their nationalistic pride along with their traditions, ideologies, and values. Even those who keep their nationalistic ways and refuse to adapt to the West continue to live in the psychic space of "borderville" (e.g., hatred toward their adopted country).

Therefore, I have taken the liberty to expand on the borderline disorder, describing eight different kinds of borderline personality disorders along with specific kinds of communication techniques and methods: The eight different types of borderlines are (1) the Pathological Borderline, (2) the Malignant Borderline, (3) the Depressive Borderline, (4) the Obsessive–Compulsive Borderline (the Pack Rat/the Addict), (5) the Antisocial Borderline, (6) the Passive–Aggressive Borderline, (7) the Histrionic Borderline, and (8) the Cross-Cultural Borderline (touches on our current global homeland security concerns—for example, the terrorist).

The objective of this book is to offer new approaches to communicating with, working with, and treating borderline personality disorders while integrating more contemporary approaches into our treatment methods. Thus, there will be numerous case examples offered within each chapter, and the book will also touch on the kinds of partners that borderlines attract. It offers guidelines for special communication for each type of borderline, including the cross-cultural borderline. For example, what dependency means to a Westerner may have an entirely different meaning to someone who is Japanese (*amae*), and the way one addresses needs or the concept of self to an Asian is quite different from how one would approach the subject to a Westerner.

> *What do you mean you want to help me develop a self? In Japan we do not have a "self." We belong to a family, a group, a society and we must be careful not to shame them!*

Our waiting rooms are beginning to look like a mini-United Nations, especially with multicultural couples, ethnic couples, and interracial couples representing evermore diverse ethnic backgrounds. More research needs to be done in this area, because those from other nations bring with them their nationalist flags and beliefs, along with an entirely different array of dynamics.

Treating cross-cultural couples has provided the need for greater in-depth understanding of couples with assorted ethnic backgrounds and their varying psychodynamics. With this comes an entire array of cultural traditions, customs, and a nationalistic pride that cannot adapt to nor or tolerate the other partner's ideologies or beliefs. I think that what makes this book unique is examining issues surrounding cruelty and aggression from a psychological, cultural, and psychohistorical perspective that runs the gamut from the domestic to the global (case examples will be given).

The book begins by introducing the reader to the borderline personality disorder, along with the challenges and difficulties it presents to clinicians. I then explain the complexity of understanding this syndrome by offering various theoretical perspectives, ranging from Freud to current treatment modalities including Marsha Linehan's innovative Dialectic Behavioral Therapy approach. Throughout this book, I ask the reader to be aware of contrasting concepts and to think of the borderline within the language of dialectics, with each of the eight borderline personalities requiring specific communication techniques and methods. For instance, to the Antisocial Borderline the therapist might say,

Your only concern is that you got caught; yet you don't seem to have compassion for your wife who had to sit and wait five years while you served your jail sentence.

Whereas to the obsessive–compulsive, the therapist might say,

Your only concern is that you have to be perfect, and when you are not you feel messy and dirty inside. Therefore, you continually wash your hands or clean out your file drawers because you think emotions and vulnerability are messy and dirty.

Talking and communicating with a borderline is not an easy task. When speaking with a borderline one must watch every word, every gesture, and always walk on thin ice (Mason, 1998). It makes us feel like we are "walking on eggs," and that they are the "eggs." They are "egoless." If you step on a borderline, they crack, for they are ever so fragile and easily hooked into what I have described in one of my earlier contributions as "the V-spot" (Lachkar, 2008a). "The V-Spot" is a term I created to describe the area of intense emotional vulnerability that stems from early childhood trauma, an area so explosive that one dare not trespass. Even the most innocuous remark can make the person blow. In psychoanalytic terms this is known as the archaic injury. "He/she really stirred up my V-spot," is a concept far more graspable to the average person than the term "archaic injury" (especially useful when talking to borderlines who often disassociate or split off from their internal world). All of us have had the experience of saying something in a rather matter-of-fact way and suddenly being attacked for an innocuous comment not intended to be hurtful or injurious. We also know this as "pushing one's buttons," or as I say (Lachkar, 2008), succinctly titles it head-on in his book *Walking on Eggshells:*

What do you mean when you say you didn't understand what I said? Are you calling me a liar?

How does knowledge of the V-spot help? What has this got to do with communicating with a borderline? The V-spot is an important link to "ego functions." When the ego gets flooded or overwhelmed or the V-spot gets stirred, the first thing that goes is the ability to think. Judgment, perception, and reality are impaired. When this occurs, the borderline goes into "ego dysfunctionality." "When you are feeling such rage toward your boss, it is best not to make any decisions about quitting your job!" As one patient, the partner of a borderline, recounts, "The only way I became a borderline survivor was when I began to understand his special language.

I never knew how to respond to the absurdity. Yes means no and no means yes, wait a minute means never, to have a fun thing planned means sabotage!" Linehan reinforces the notion that the "validating," nonjudgmental environment offers an opportunity to regulate affect and self-soothe.

Even though they seemingly have their own idiosyncratic nature, borderlines do share personality traits with other disorders. Nevertheless, they all seem to have been fertilized in the same Petri dish. Diagnostically stated, the most dominant features are low self-esteem, loss of ego identity, suicide ideation, impulsivity, acting out, inflicting harm on self/others, persecutory anxieties, abandonment/betrayal, distorted sense of dependency, victimization, intense rage, and paranoid ideation. Many have lived in their own inner isolated world, especially those children with early traumatic childhoods—e.g., alcoholic parents, parents who either physically or emotionally abandoned them, children whose childhoods necessitated that they be parentified children, caretakers to their own parents. These are the "little adults" who grew up much too early and much too soon.

Outline of the Book

Chapter 1 contains an overview of the borderline and assesses this disorder with reference to many diagnostic approaches that extend beyond the DSM-IV. It also lists and discusses the relative ego strengths and weakness of the borderline based on the relative intactness of reality, thought processes, and interpersonal relatedness.

Chapter 2 revisits many of the classical theoretical approaches, and introduces some of the newer ones. It attempts to unravel the complexity involved in understanding the borderline from various theoretical perspectives. It also addresses the confusion resulting from the many variations on the theme of borderlines. The essence of our new postmodern borderline is viewed through the eyes of different clinicians.

Chapter 3 introduces the pathological borderline. This chapter focuses on communicating with this least toxic type of borderline. Pathological borderlines generally are not physically abusive or outwardly sadistic. However, they are manipulative, clingy, overly dependent, and will do anything to bond with their objects through pain and victimization. They have a cult-like mentality, are dominated by primitive defenses such as shame, splitting, projection, and envy. They want to dominate and tend to consume and take over their love relations.

Chapter 4 describes the malignant borderline, who is similar to the malignant narcissist but with extreme paranoid and antisocial features. This type of borderline is the most flagrant, malicious, and abusive, and the source of domestic violence and global terrorism. They are basically evil, with no sense of conscience or morality, and are pathological liars, manipulators, abusers. They suffer from lack of trust and maliciously distort the good intentions of others. Often they are cult-like or tyrannical leaders such as Slobodan Milosevic, Saddam Hussein, or Osama bin Laden.

Chapter 5 examines the depressive borderline. This type of borderline uses his depression as a false means of bonding with his objects through victimization, persecutory anxiety, and self-hatred. These are the borderlines who not only feel the pain or the paralysis; they become the pain or the paralysis. This is almost a reverse narcissist, a person so depleted of external supplies that they resort to turning inward.

Chapter 6 focuses on the obsessive–compulsive borderline and their next-door neighbors in borderland—the collector, the pack rat, and the addict. These personalities are consumed by their objects or their addictions. They regard their internal emotional life as filthy and dirty and bond with objects as replacements for love and intimacy.

Chapter 7 highlights the antisocial borderline, whose serious superego defect allows no capacity for empathy, remorse, or guilt for their wrongdoings. They present a more severe pathology than the narcissist, even though they both display a grandiose self and exaggerated sense of entitlement.

Chapter 8 examines the passive–aggressive borderline: This type is one of the most difficult to treat for they are always trying to recreate the parent/child dyad. They are the procrastinators, the ones who will always "do it later" or tomorrow, although tomorrow never comes.

Chapter 9 focuses on the histrionic borderline—someone who cries easily, has excessive parasitic dependency needs, and displays emotionality on his or her sleeve. In some instances the histrionic borderline may appear very narcissistic, but they use their powers seductively, not necessarily to feel special but as a way of provocatively bonding with their objects.

Chapter 10 discusses the cross-cultural borderline: This chapter ranges from domestic abuse to global terrorism, examining how cross-cultural borderlines not only bring to their new country and to their relationships a certain nationalistic pride, but how they vehemently and relentlessly persuade others to become "believers." Those who do not comply with their beliefs become the betrayers or the "infidels." In relationships, they cannot adapt to or tolerate the other partner's political or religious views.

Chapter 11 contains closing thoughts that reflect on the ever-changing landscape of our clinical practices and reiterating communication styles applicable to the various types of borderlines described in this book. As we choreograph our "dance of words," we must prepare ourselves to meet the constant challenges the borderline presents not only in our consultation rooms, but in the world around us.

1

The Borderline
An Overview

This chapter focuses on assessing borderline personality disorder. It extends the criteria in *The Diagnostic and Statistical Manual of Mental Disorders* (DSM-IV) to include the borderline's relative ego strengths and weaknesses, based on the degree of intactness of reality testing, thought processes, and the ability to maintain and sustain impersonal relations in an object relational world. Since the publication of DSM-IV (see Table of Diagnostic Approaches in the Appendix), many authors and clinicians—including Kernberg (1985a), Gunderson (1984), Linehan (1993a), Lachkar (2008b)—have contributed to and expanded the description of the borderline personality.

The main dynamic of the borderline personality disorder is abandonment anxiety. Like codependents, borderlines attempt to preempt or prevent abandonment (both real and imagined) by their nearest and dearest. They cling frantically and counterproductively to their partners, mates, spouses, friends, children, and others. This fierce attachment is coupled with idealization and then swift and merciless devaluation of the borderline's target (Vaknim, 2007). To get a sense of self or of self-worth, or to offset a chaotic self-image, they will do anything (steal, gamble, take drugs, shop, abuse alcohol, engage in promiscuous behavior) to assuage the emptiness. Their lack of impulse control is met with self-destructive and self-defeating behaviors such as suicide threats, self-mutilation, and other acts to counteract the aching pain of aloneness and isolation. The list of borderline traits and characteristics that appears below is based on a pervasive pattern of loneliness, feelings of deprivation, shame, self-persecution, and abandonment anxiety. I have taken the liberty of including these characteristics in the list, which offers a more definitive composite of borderline personality disorder, beginning with some of the relative ego strength and weakness criteria.

Ego strengths of borderlines include the relative intactness of:

- Reality testing
- Thought processes
- Interpersonal relations
- Adaptation to reality

Underlying ego weaknesses of borderlines include:

- The combination of poor impulse control, impatience, and poor frustration tolerance.
- The proclivity to use primitive ego defenses (splitting, projection, projective identification, magical thinking).
- Affective instability.
- Identity diffusion.
- A pervasive pattern of instability of mood, troubled interpersonal relationships, and poor self-image, beginning by early adulthood and present in a variety of contexts, as indicated by at least five of the following symptoms:
  - A frantic effort to avoid real or imagined abandonment.
  - Intensely disturbed interpersonal relationships characterized by alternating between extremes of idealization and devaluation.
  - Identity disturbance, markedly and persistently unstable self-image or sense of self.
  - Impulsivity in at least two areas that are potentially self-damaging (e.g., out-of-control spending, insatiable sex, substance abuse, reckless driving, binge-eating).
  - Recurrent suicidal behavior, gestures, threats, or self-mutilating behavior.
  - Affective instability stemming from a marked reactivity of mood (e.g., intense episodic dysphoria, irritability, or anxiety usually lasting a few hours and only rarely more than a few days).
  - Inappropriate affect, outbursts of anger, or difficulty controlling emotions (e.g., frequent displays of temper, constant anger, recurrent physical fights).
  - A history of emotional and physical abuse.

- Never separating from mother's body. Many borderlines remained fused with the maternal object and confuse sexuality with love and intimacy. In love relationships, they often will become the "Don Juans," or "femme fatales" (Marilyn Monroe, Madonna), as their confused sexual identity offers them a pretext to be sexually alluring.
- Bonding with pain; difficulty in early attachment bonding relations.
- Hypersensitivity to criticism or rejection. Feeling of "needing" someone else to survive; constant need for validation and reassurance.
- Hard time controlling and regulating their emotions; emotions have a stranglehold on them.
- Chronic feelings of emptiness or boredom (the black hole), an emptiness so pervasive that it seemingly can never be filled, but in an attempt to try to fill it, they become insatiable. "More drugs! More sex! More cuts on my wrists!"
- A "false self" that belies the "true self," marked by persistent identity disturbance, including shifts in self-image, sexual orientation, career choices, or other long-term goals.
- A preoccupation with what people think; taking on a chameleon-like self to please people.
- A neediness to find someone in order to survive, which contributes to chaotic, intense relationships characterized by splitting (fluctuations between love and hate).
- Victimization often accompanied by psychosomatic illness (bond with their objects through pain as the replacement for love).
- Problems with object constancy; difficulty with separation causes them to fuse with the object because they cannot hold onto or recreate the image or memory of the object.

Borderlines also have some very good qualities. Because of their heightened sensitivity and vulnerability, they are extremely creative and artistic (Beethoven, Picasso, Van Gogh, Michael Jackson, Madonna, Marilyn Monroe, and Britney Spears). Often they become super good friends, are entertaining, amusing, complimentary, very perceptive, and sensitive.

As a preface to discussing the eight different kinds of borderlines in the following chapters and exploring how best to communicate with them, I am including a mental status exam (Table 1.1). This exam is useful in determining the diagnostic distinctions and facilitating communication.

How do we know we are in the presence of a borderline? Many say the experience is like nothing else. Some people are completely charmed and

TABLE 1.1
Mental Status Exam Criteria

Characteristic	Traits	Example
Appearance	Uncaring about basic health, hygiene, hair, teeth, cleanliness, appropriate dress according to age range, profession, genre, or lifestyle.	A therapist might have a hard time telling the patient about the holes in his shirt and pants, but when the time is right, the therapist can link the holes to the patient's internal experience. "You are letting us know by the holes in your clothes how empty and disconnected you feel."
Attitude	Arrogant, aggressive, submissive, cooperative, argumentative, hostile, guarded, suspicious/paranoid.	"It is difficult at this point for you to make any major decisions or changes in your life when your moods are so changeable" (ego dysfunctionality).
Cognition	Difficulties with memory, ability to organize the data of experience, ability to organize thought in a cohesive manner.	"It is hard to remember when so much shame/blame/guilt and persecutory anxiety is operative. This makes it difficult to trust your mind and make decisions."
Behavior	Abnormalities in movement, gait, eye contact, body language, focus, hesitation. A person who walks into the office and glances around as if he/she is being followed gives an indication of paranoia or paranoid anxiety.	A man walks into the office and sees two chairs. Even though he was told where to sit with a gesture, he hesitates.
Mood and affect	Changeable from being apologetic to aggressive.	"When your friend called and cancelled her plans with you, you attacked her and told her to get the hell out of your life. You thought you were expressing your feelings. You were confusing your feelings (defenses) with aggression."
Speech	Lack of clarity, articulation, focus, spontaneity, expression, coherency, tone, articulation.	"I am here to help you communicate because sometimes I find that you hesitate."

TABLE 1.1 (CONTINUED) Mental Status Exam Criteria		
Characteristic	Traits	Example
Thought process	Many different levels: confusion and difficulty organizing experiential data, flight or slowness of ideas, repetition of thoughts and ideas, fragmentation, inhibition of thoughts, withholding thoughts (very common with borderlines, who hide behind the shame); other aspects relate to flow, associations, time taken to express a thought, open-ended thoughts, illogical and irrational thoughts, phobias, delusional or obsessive thoughts, preoccupation, and ruminations.	Borderlines can worry that they may have forgotten to turn off the stove even when they know they always check things over and over again.
Perceptions	Trouble reading body language of others, distortions, delusions, illusions, hallucinations.	"You are so used to being abandoned and betrayed that you think when I go on vacation that I am doing what your parents did, trying to get away from you. Actually, my vacation has nothing to do with you. It is about me and my needs."
Insight	Lack of ability to predict and make sense of what is happening, of using one's judgment; preconception of ideas.	"You are so quick to take in the negative projections of others that it interferes with your ability to pay attention to your inner voice" (preconceptions/intuition).
Judgment	Inability to make sound, reasonable, responsible decisions, not based on impulse but with self-awareness and the capacity to anticipate and plan ahead.	"When you are in the shame/blame phase of your relationship, it is best not to make any decisions at that time."

(Continued)

	TABLE 1.1 (CONTINUED) Mental Status Exam Criteria		

Characteristic	*Traits*	*Example*
Cultural considerations	Need to distinguish cultural beliefs from delusions and hallucinations; need to take into consideration the person's language, culture, racial and educational background.	"In this country men are not allowed to beat up their wives. However, they can say, 'I feel like beating up my wife or stoning her.' But they are not allowed to do it."
Good qualities	Often do quite well professionally; frequently are artistic, creative, perceptive, and desire to bond and make close attachments; have an unusually high degree of interpersonal sensitivity, heightened awareness, insight, and empathy.	"Others may find you weird and strange. I find you to be very creative, artistic, and unique."

blown away by the borderline's charisma, outgoing persona, and jubilant personality. "I really like this person; he gives me the sense he is really into me!" Others describe the experience as strange and bizarre, but cannot quite pinpoint exactly what the strangeness is. "What is she talking about? Why is she just babbling on and on? Why did she get so upset?" Frequently, borderlines are anti-establishment and rebel against the demands society puts on them. "Why should I dress up to go to the opera? It's only a bunch of people screeching at the top of their lungs!"

Borderlines got their name because they lack "boundaries"—not because they do not want them but because they are felt to be too threatening. Most borderlines come from enmeshed family environments (or what Linehan refers to as "the invalidating environment"), with parents that did not offer good structure, discipline, or limits when their children were growing up. Closely linked with the borderline's confused sense of identity, stemming from the lack of boundaries, is identity diffusion, whereby the borderline thinks he or she has sufficiently separated from the maternal object by physically or even geographically moving away or acting and living independently from her. However, unbeknownst to the borderline, fragments of the ties to the maternal object remain insidiously hidden. Borderlines are very polarized because of their nonintegrated self and often see the world as all good or all bad. If they internalize the object-mother as all bad, they will project the bad mother onto people that they meet and interact with and, therefore, become unable to balance the negative with the positive.

I recall doing a workshop for divorce lawyers and mediators. The focus was on the impossible clients who go through the mediation process constantly bickering and blaming without ever reaching any conflict resolution. Even when "good advice" is offered, they fail to take heed. I will never forget one attorney with a Germanic accent, who stood up, frantically waved her arms, and shouted. "Boundaries! Boundaries! Boundaries are everything! *Boundaries*" (having had a German mother, I could certainly relate).

This lack of boundaries takes many forms. I remember a feeling of ominous foreboding when the phone rang one day. I just knew it was she. "Hello! Dr. Lachkar, I just want you to know I am on my way!" I sit and wait and wait, and, as I predicted, the phone rings again. Sure enough, I hear a jubilant voice at the other end, "Hi! It's me again. Just want you to know I will be about ten minutes late! See you soon!" Again, I wait. I stare at the phone waiting for it to ring and wonder when it does if I should pick it up or just contain. Why does she put me through this? I become preoccupied thinking about what I will say to her. Do I point out her inappropriate behavior, or do I welcome her and show that I am pleased to see her? Why am I walking on eggshells? Why am I so preoccupied with what to say?

Talking to a borderline means timing: the ability to recognize in advance when the blow-up is about to occur. For example, a histrionic borderline patient, who is an actress, got very disturbed about something I said. As I spoke, I had an immediate impulse to stop or change the subject, but it was too late. I had gone past the point of no return. Intuitively I felt that I was pushing her vulnerable spot, her V-spot (Lachkar, 2008a). I had an ominous feeling that I was about to be attacked by some strange alien. The next thing I knew she stormed out of the room. My immediate reaction was that I had lost her and she would never return. I refrained from calling her thereafter. When she returned for her next session, my immediate reaction was to discuss the incident with her. Instead, appealing to her dramatic side, I played on the fact that she was an actor and commented, "Ah, the artist is back! What a performance!" When she realized that I did not respond to her as the "bad child," we were able to process the occurrence (not acceptance but a transitional moment). She laughed and was pleased that I was not angry with her but could accept her experience as a momentary explosion, and that it did not take away from the importance of her treatment. In a way, I was glad it happened, because by pushing her V-spot, I was able to understand more about her own histrionic mother who would get out of control. It also was reassuring to both of us to know that I could maintain my role and be accessible to help this patient.

This little vignette says it all: the ability to play and communicate creatively with our borderline patients. At that moment, I am the Winnicottian "playful" mommy, as opposed to the out-of-control or persecutory one. This experience addresses the borderline's many primitive defenses and ego weaknesses (lack of impulse control, lack of identity, inability to mentalize, primitive splitting, projection, and projective identification). Mentalization is described later in this book but, briefly, it refers to Bion's concept of an unborn thought, a thoughtless thought, a thought that has not yet been experienced, or as Bion so aptly describes it, as "a thought without a thinker."

CASE OF TOM: INITIAL INTERVIEW

Tom's appointment was at 11:00 a.m. He called three times to tell me he would be late. I waited and waited, seeing patients in between. He finally showed up at 5:00 p.m. He told me he had gone to the wrong building, had difficulty parking, and that, when he got off the elevator, he had to go to the bathroom, but the door was locked, so he went downstairs to the coffee shop (keys to the bathroom are in my waiting room). As we began our initial session, he mentioned he was worried about his car because he saw a cop put a ticket on his windshield. When I asked where he parked, he said he couldn't find a spot and got so frustrated he parked in the alley. I immediately had him move his car and mentioned I would wait. He came back, telling me what bastards those cops were to give him a ticket. Surprisingly, he was willing to work and wasted no time expressing his rage and frustrations about his family and, mainly, how he felt he was wrongly hospitalized.

Tom was referred by a friend who was the relative of a very well-known movie director. It was intriguing for me to study the types of individuals who come from families with so much fame and wealth yet produce children with BPD. Even though I knew this patient was going to be quite a challenge, my interest and curiosity overcame my doubts. As treatment progressed, I was surprised that Tom began to show up closer and closer to the appointment time, and in some cases even arrived early. Tom would do fine for a while. However, if I ever mentioned that there was a defect within him that caused other people to respond to him the way they do, he would counter with uncontrollable rage. "How dare you say that! You are fucked up just like everyone else. My parents did bad things to me, and it is their entire fault. If it weren't for them, I would have a nice life and wouldn't be sitting here talking to you!"

Therapist (Th): So, you blame your parents for all your problems?

Tom (T): Yes, my mother used to throw me against the wall and do all kinds of bad things to me.

Th: Then you were abused? Where was your father?

T: He did nothing, the asshole.

Th: So, in a way you are like your mother. When you get angry you become abusive.

T: I am not abusive, and don't you dare tell me I am like my mother!

Th: You're right. You are not like your mother. Your mother would never go to therapy to get help. At least you are here, and I commend you for that.

T: Oh, yeah. I guess that's good.

Th: Even the way you get angry is different from your mother.

T: Like how?

Th: The cops got "angry" with you for parking in the wrong space, but they were doing their job. Your mother got angry with you because she did not do her job. She did not have the parenting skills to discipline her child (fusion with the "bad, unjust cop mother").

T: No, she was an idiot who didn't know from nothing.

Th: So, basically, a little while ago we were not talking about where you parked your car. We were talking about boundary confusion: what you did, what the cops did, and what your mother did. She was your mother, but she didn't act as a mother should. Just as parking in an alley is not the same as parking in a space provided for cars (the language of dialectics).

T: Wow! This is great. I never thought about this before.

Th: I see you have analytic insights. Tom. This can be very helpful to us. I am impressed. We have to stop now. See you next time.

T: Why do we have to stop? It was not my fault I was late.

Th: But if I continue and my next patient comes, then I would be "parking" in the wrong space. Just like the car: what is your space and what is mine.

T: Okay, got it. See you next week.

Th: Good work, Tom.

An Invitation to the Dance

*Choreographing the Endless Round of Primitive
Defenses and Regressive Behaviors*

Throughout my publications, I have referred to the metaphor of "the dance" to describe the introjective/projective process that occurs when one partner projects a negative feeling onto the other, and how the other then tends to identify or overidentify with that which is being projected. Couples go round and round in a never-ending pattern without ever reaching any conflict resolution (Lachkar, 1992, 2008b). For example, in *The Narcissistic/Borderline Couple* I describe how the circular, rondo-like patterns of the partners become a dance between envy and jealousy, between the guilt projected by the narcissist and the shame projected by the borderline. In *How to Talk to a Narcissist,* I describe eight different kinds of narcissists and their dynamics, with the sole purpose of helping therapists formulate specific ways to communicate with someone who is totally absorbed with self. Within the matrix of the borderline dance, I do the same, showing how each type of borderline brings to the psychological stage his or her own qualitative experience.

The case that follows illustrates how many of the elements involved in BPD (abandonment, issues around separation, victimization, fusion with the maternal object) create the dance between borderlines and those who enter their sphere.

The Case of Bill and Sara

Now I know who I am! I am a borderline!

THE "WE COUPLE" AND THE LANGUAGE OF DIALECTICS

Bill complains that Sara ignores, abandons, and does not want to do things with him as a couple. "I want to be an 'us' and a 'we,' and Sara wants to do her own thing. She asked me to clean out the garage and move the clutter, which I did not do because I did not have time. Then she started to point her finger at me the same way my mother did. This is when I blew up! I went into an uncontrollable rage. I belong to a BPD group, and know that I am a borderline and have been told that this is what borderlines do!" Sara, not knowing how to confront Bill or understand his impulsive outburst, internalizes Bill's rage and goes into a depression. This is her self-hatred turned inward. "I feel so guilty. He wants me around all the time, so that we can be a couple, and I need my space."

As their couple therapist, I felt that this was my moment to intervene and explain to Bill that his desire for closeness and intimacy is healthy and natural, but in reality he is not asking for closeness. In a very soft voice, I say, "But, Bill, instead of asking for closeness with your wife, you are asking for fusion with a long-ago-abandoned maternal attachment that you seek to resurrect now." He looked at me in shock and said, "This is news to me. I have never heard that before! My mother never did things with me. She always went her own way."

I could already see the beginning of "the dance" (Lachkar, 2008), and how Bill projects his deprived and rejected self toward Sara, and how Sara identifies with his negative projections in a self-persecutory way, which then leads to depression. Here is an illustration of the therapist's use of the "language of dialectics" as she moves back and forth in harmony with the "dance." These are movements between fusion/merging and separation/interdependency. The more Bill projects and threatens, the more Sara withdraws; the more she withdraws, the more he attacks and loses contact with the "we/us" couple. What a bitter paradox! The very thing that borderlines crave is the very thing they destroy.

It is amazing how the various theoretical positions—ranging from the classical to the most contemporary—invite, embrace, and direct us into the type of communication style we select. In the case of Bill and Sara, Bill complains that Sara continually makes him feel guilty for avoiding intimacy. At this moment, the therapist can hear Klein's voice saying, "Bill, this sounds like legitimate guilt and a good reason to feel guilty, and we need to take a look at what kind of feelings intimacy evokes in you." Then the therapist may hear Kohut's voice calling out in the background and think, "Hey, wait a minute, Klein! Where is the empathy?" To this, a Kohutian therapist might respond, "I can understand why you avoid intimacy, since it makes you feel too vulnerable and needy." Sara says that she feels guilty for making Bill feel guilty. To this Klein retorts, "This is not your guilt. You are overidentifying with Bill's guilt." Kohut then reappears and says, "How could you allow yourself to be intimate when your mother was cold and never hugged or embraced you?" This is mirroring the experience. Klein returns with her harsh reality to Sara and says, "You are distorting! You are projecting! Your primitive defenses and boundary confusion get in the way of seeing how you internalize Bill's guilt, thus leaving you with a distorted sense of reality!" Kohut cannot resist replying, "What do you mean, a distorted sense of reality? Sara has her own subjective experience of reality, and you cannot tell her that she distorts her reality." We then hear a newer and younger voice enter the picture. It is Marsha Linehan. "Hold on! This couple is in reactive, not cognitive, mode. Allow them to stay for a while in the state of mindlessness. You are moving too fast." Welcome to the language of dialectics!

Primitive Defenses and Psychodynamics

Not only is there a dance between the couple; there is also a dance between their psychodynamics.

The most pervasive dynamics within the borderline structure are the movements between guilt/shame, envy/jealousy, domination/submission, omnipotence/dependency, idealization/devaluation, and attachment/detachment. The most dominant dynamics are shame and envy as the borderline invites and is constantly subjected to the negative projections of others.

Shame Versus Guilt

In order to communicate with a borderline, we first must differentiate between shame and guilt. Shame is one of the most common defenses and surfaces repeatedly in couples therapy. Shame is often equated with neediness. Guilt, on the other hand, represents a higher form of development than shame and has an internal punitive voice that operates at the level of the superego. It occurs in the depressive position, followed by the desire to make reparation and confess transgressions or wrongdoings. Shame is associated with isolation and being abandoned by the group or society. Guilt is a reaction against an act of doing and remorse for that act (Lansky, 1987), while shame is the preoccupation with what others think. Shame is reactive (as well as cultural) and is very difficult to recognize. When someone has been living in shame for an entire lifetime, it is exceedingly difficult to suddenly be forced to face that which cannot be faced. Much to their surprise, the very shame that they have been hiding is the same shame that is their treasure.

Mrs. L. felt her needs were demanding and cumbersome. She feared that, if she asked too many questions and called between sessions when she was feeling desperate, she would be a big burden. She had a dream that she was digging a hole in her backyard and, much to her surprise, instead of finding dirt, moles, and rats, she found a huge wealth of jewels (gold, diamonds, rubies).

Even readers who are not therapists can easily interpret this dream—that Mrs. L. felt her inner world was filled with weighty piles of dirt that would be too cumbersome for her therapy to handle. But, in reality, when she confronts the shame she discovers her needs, desires, and feelings to be precious treasures.

According to Kernberg (1975), borderlines lack the capacity to experience guilt. The demands of the superego are felt to be so intense that, instead of responding to the moral voices of the superego, projection and splitting become the psychic alternative. "I must get rid of these bad feelings!"

The following scenarios of two men caught having affairs illustrate why therapists need to distinguish between shame and guilt in their communication style.

Example One: The wife finds her husband's cell phone (what she refers to as "the fuck phone") with text and phone messages from other women. The day of reckoning comes. She confronts him. His first response is to attack her and make her feel that she is making things up, that she is delusional (attack and persecutory anxiety as the replacement for guilt and remorse).

Example Two: The wife finds her husband's cell phone with voice and text messages, as well as hotel and restaurant receipts. She confronts him. At first he denies and later comes clean about this break of trust, asks forgiveness, and makes an appointment with a therapist (normal guilt with desire for reparation).

The True and False Self

A face prepared to meet the faces that you meet.

—T. S. Elliot

Winnicott refers to borderlines as those who exhibit a false self, a pseudo self, a persona that belies the true self. As outlined in the list presented earlier in the chapter, theirs is a marked, persistent identity disturbance that includes shifts in self-image, sexual orientation, career choices, or other long-term goals. They are overly concerned with what other people think and often take on a chameleon-like self to please others. "I'll be whatever you want me to be; please don't leave me!" For a while they can perform the role of a "people pleaser," the compliant self, but it is short lived. Soon lack of impulse control rears its ugly head and all is lost. I refer to this as the Zelig Syndrome (Woody Allen's movie, 1983).

Since they lack a "real self," borderlines must invent an imaginary one to attract or seduce others. Often they are the Don Juans, the femme fatales, who operate through seduction, charm, and charisma. They promise the world and then let down and disappoint. Their convincing tones and personality can dupe even the most emotionally attuned person (Lachkar, 2008b). Typically, pathological borderlines choose people like narcissists, a person who plays into the borderline's false self or compliant self. "You are the most wonderful, beautiful woman in the world. I will do anything for you!" For a short while, a borderline can pretend to perform the role of being the perfect mirroring self-object for the narcissist, but because of the lack of impulse control, the borderline partner cannot sustain this and eventually lashes out.

> I feel so stupid. Why didn't I trust my true feelings? I got duped into believing she was the woman of my dreams. When I first met her, she was so sexy, charming, loving, and willing to do anything and everything. Now she sleeps all day, takes drugs, can't hold a job, and never wants anything to do with sex.

One man, a musician, could not understand why his girlfriend told him that Shostakovich was her favorite composer and "when we went to hear his symphony she thought she was going to faint from the diatonic sounds. Why couldn't she just admit it and not put on this pretense for me?"

Envy Versus Jealousy

Klein made a distinction between envy and jealousy. Envy is a part-object function and is not based on love. It is destructive in nature and is considered to be the most primitive and fundamental emotion. Its intent is to destroy that which is envied. Jealousy, unlike envy, is a triangular relationship based on love, wherein one desires to be part of the family, group, or nation. Jealousy reflects a higher form of development than envy. It is a whole-object relationship that desires the object but does not seek to destroy it or perceive the other as an oedipal rival (those who take mother away).

Domination Versus Submission

Domination is a form of projective identification in which the object is forced either consciously or unconsciously to yield to the will of the other person. The person who is controlled or dominated often moves into a form of masochistic surrender and gives up his/her own needs to satisfy and glorify the other. This is a part-object relationship in which the object does not seek to destroy the other but to subjugate part of the self that goes into submission and a state of victimization, the role of the enabler.

Omnipotence Versus Dependency

The discussion of omnipotence and dependency is crucial, because borderlines often have difficulty forming healthy dependency relations since they feel their needs are dangerous and persecutory. Children whose formative years are deficient in maternal care-taking grow up never learning how to develop healthy bonding attachments. To ward off intolerable feelings of smallness and helplessness, the child grows up with a fantasy that it is bad to have needs, and will therefore project the "needy" self onto others. "It is you that is the needy one, the disgusting one, not me!" Omnipotence is the flip side of dependency. The omnipotent ones are those who do not need or want anything because they have it all. "I don't need you, I don't need your advice, and I don't need this treatment." One patient recounts that whenever he asked his mother for something (a toy, baseball cards), she would respond, "Grow up, son; big boys don't beg."

Attachment Versus Detachment

Attachment theory is based on the work of John Bowlby (1969), one of the first to recognize the importance of early ties to maternal caretakers. He observed that when children are raised in abusive or deprived environments, severe disruptions with bonding occur. The loss of the object is accompanied by the infant's increasing signs of helplessness, hopelessness, and despair. When this occurs, the infant goes into detachment mode or pathological mourning. Apathy, lethargy, and listlessness become replacements for affective experience (anger, rage, envy, betrayal, and abandonment). Detachment is not to be confused with denial and withdrawal. Bowlby stresses that, when one withdraws, one still maintains a certain libidinal tie to the object; however, when one detaches, one goes into a state of despondency. Children who are left alone or are neglected over long periods of time enter into a phase of despair.

Projection and Projective Identification

Projection is a one-way process, while projective identification is a two-way process (see below). The concept of projection is a fascinating one and offers a vast array of opportunities to communicate with a borderline in a way that can be heard and understood—through the "language of dialectics." The following dialectic reminds me of the old analytic adage that whenever someone is talking about someone else they are really talking about themselves.

> *Sally says that her boyfriend, Mike, an audio nautical engineer, is the most brilliant man she's ever met. He is perfect, except he is a shopaholic, obsessed with classic cars, objects d'art, and antique furniture. He can never have enough, despite the problem of where to store the stuff. "There is no room for me!" He makes a great deal of money, but at the end of the year he is practically broke.*

Meanwhile, Sally complains she does not have quality friends and does not feel good enough about herself to seek them out. Through the language of dialectics, I let Sally know that, on the one hand, she is talking about Mike, but on the other she is talking about a hidden part of herself that stores her internal treasures and will not let them out.

> *Sally, you are the real pack rat. You are the one who has real treasures, internal treasures that can't be bought, that you store up and don't make use of.*

Melanie Klein's (1975) invaluable formulations of projective identification have been most useful for individual and couple therapy alike. Her introjective/projective process helps therapists decipher how certain behaviors and interactions get transported back and forth. Projective identification is a two-way process wherein one tries to get rid of some negative, unwanted part of him/herself and project it onto the other, who then tends to identify or overidentify with that which is being projected. Often this can be the most confusing and delusional aspect that most people contend with when attempting to communicate with a borderline. In conjoint treatment, for example, we see how certain dynamic mechanisms of the borderline can arouse states of chaos, confusion, and terror in others, as well as shame, blame, envy, abandonment, chaos, and persecutory anxieties.

Why is it that everything she is and does she says I do? She lies and tells me I lie. She has been unfaithful, and she tells me she can't trust me! She is late and tells me I am late. She doesn't answer me when I speak, and she says I don't answer her.

These distorted accusations or vestigial remains of the past get recycled and ultimately destroy relationships.

Seeking an Identity

Hello! I am a Borderline.

It is amazing how many e-mails and messages I get, "Hello, Dr. Lachkar, I am John, and I am a borderline!" Another will call and say something like, "Hello, Dr. Lachkar! I am Sara, and my husband is a borderline!" Or "Hello, Dr. Lachkar! My name is Veronica. I am a borderline, and my husband is the narcissist." What follows is a letter that typifies this current trend to identity disturbance, with a markedly and persistently unstable self-image or sense of self. (See letter below.) These individuals will often resort to a negative identity rather than none at all.

Finding an identity is a universal concept. The major difference between a narcissist and a borderline, as described in my previous contributions, is that the narcissist already has an identity. They know they exist, but are in constant search for a "special" identity. On the other hand, the borderline could care less about being "special" but is concerned with proving he or she exists as a thing in itself (Lachkar, 2004b, 2008a, 2008b). Extending beyond the clinical to the global world, we are witness to terrorists who commit the most heinous crimes against humanity, but do so because it gives meaning and purpose to the meaningless. In interviews with suicide bombers, even those who resisted death succumbed for the "greater cause" and expressed they felt this gave meaning and purpose to their lives and honor to their family.

Ironically, borderline personalities think they are coming for treatment for a cure, but they are really in a quest to create meaning out of the meaninglessness (Grotstein, 1987). "Now I know who I am. I am a borderline!" What follows is an amalgam of the numerous letters and correspondence I receive.

My name is Emily, and I am married to a malignant borderline. I need you to help me find a therapist in my hometown of Missouri or a tele-communication group to help me in this mentally abusive relationship. We have been married for 10 years, and from the beginning I knew there was something off about him. He always seemed to be in good humor, laughing, joking, making light of things, but later that started to wear off. His true self began to emerge. He became a womanizer, verbally and emotionally abusive to our two daughters and me. When I disagreed with him or had a differing opinion, he would call me a cunt or a bitch and bad-mouth me in front of the kids. Whenever I con-fronted him, he would become even more cruel and sadistic.

Upon reading about the borderline disorder, I was blown away to find out I was not alone, that this kind of abusive relationship with borderlines truly exists. At first I felt like I was going crazy and never thought I could get into an abusive relationship. I was always on the alert to watch for the red flags, but with this guy, he had a great cover. He completely duped me, was ever so charming, and made me feel as though I was the only woman in the whole world. What kills me is that he still fools people. People do not believe me when I tell them he is abusive. They see him as warm, compassionate, and caring. Yet, with him I always have to walk on eggshells, and I am tired of this and desperately need help for myself and my two young daughters. Now I get it. There is a title, a name for this! Borderline! My husband is a borderline! Please, if you can help me, or you should know of someone in my area, I shall be very grateful.

My Good Friend, the Borderline: Capacity for Good Object Relations

Many borderlines lack the capacity and continuity to maintain good object relations. The splitting between good and bad and the lack of integration keeps borderlines forever threatened, lonely, and isolated. Their parasitic bonding eventually becomes the substitute for maintaining healthy friendships or love bonds. Some borderlines make the best friends; they are loyal, warm, empathic, willing to help, perceptive, and have amazing intuition. However, as soon as the friendship develops more intensely or when a needy friend begins to act more independently, the empathy and capacity for attachment diminishes.

I can't understand what happened! She was always such a good friend when I was in need, and now that I feel better she attacks me, talks about me behind my back, and acts as though I betrayed her.

Why do borderline patients manipulate? Or do they? Was Tom manipulating me by coming late and keeping me waiting? What was Tom trying to tell me? He is the quintessential example of someone reacting rather than plotting something against me. According to Linehan, the borderline does not tend to manipulate, and is more inclined to react. She describes manipulation as a deliberate thought process, a shrewd cognitive plan that is designed to fool or trick someone, whereas reactive behavior is a mindless, thoughtless process. Her description is closely aligned with what I describe as the "V-spot" (Lachkar, 2008a), which reacts explosively to imminent danger (e.g., fear/terror of abandonment, betrayal, helplessness).

What has been very liberating for many borderline patients is when the therapist helps them think beyond the black-and-white polarities and realize that there can be many realities other than their own "knee-jerk" reactions. If the therapist gazes away for a moment, borderline patients may instantly feel that the therapist has abandoned them or disapproved of something they said and may "react" by sitting through the next session with eyes looking downward. Is this a manipulation or a reaction? Sometimes it is a mixed bag. But since our focus is on communication, I would like to take Bion's (1961) concept of projective identification into consideration and react.

> *I see that now you are not looking at me. You have been looking downward during most of the session. I think you are letting me know what it felt like when I took my eyes off you and how you immediately thought you did something wrong. I averted my glance because you said something important, and I could think more clearly when I looked away.*

The next chapter reviews the various theoretical perspectives and constructs that help in our attempt to cope with borderline personality disorder.

2

Theoretical Perspectives
Looking to Our Founding Fathers

This chapter offers a description and overview of the general domain of the borderline personality and revisits many of the classical theoretical approaches, in addition to introducing some of the more contemporary ones. It attempts to unravel the complexity of understanding the borderline from various theoretical perspectives. It also addresses the confusion resulting from so many variations on the theme of borderline pathology. What is a borderline? Essentially, before we decide how to talk to a borderline, we have to come to terms with what kind of a borderline we are talking about.

The term *borderline* first appeared when discussing patients who in the beginning seemed analyzable and only later proved to offer great difficulties within the traditional analytic process. Adolph Stern first coined the term *borderline personality disorder* (BPD) in the 1930s, viewing it as a cross between Freud's cluster of psychosis and neurosis. However, for centuries, European society excluded people regarded as "insane" from normal life, confining them to asylums or driving them from one town to another. By the 18th century, a few doctors began to study the people in asylums and discovered that some of these patients had, by no means, lost the powers of reason. They had a normal grasp of what was real and what was not, although they suffered terribly from emotional anguish because of their impulsiveness, rage, and a general difficulty in self-government that caused others to suffer with them.

Because there are so many divergent views regarding the borderline personality syndrome, it is difficult to know whose borderline we are talking about. Are we dealing with a preconception of a Freudian or Kleinian borderline, a Kernbergian borderline, a Kohutian borderline, a Masterson borderline? Newer approaches include various contributions from Dialectic Behavior Therapy, mainly the innovative work of Marsha Linehan.

Many of the early classical analysts did not refer specifically to the term borderline, nor did they focus primarily on communication styles. However, the tools, techniques, and methods they used have provided us with invaluable insights. The borderline personality is not a clear and concise entity because borderline states, traits, and characteristics tend to vacillate. As one colleague remarked, "I'm not sure if my patient is narcissist or borderline, so I refer to her as a "nar/bor." Many clinicians with a psychoanalytic/psychodynamic orientation are now moving away from their couches, turning to the newer cognitive and behavioral approaches for the treatment of the borderline, including Dialectic Behavior Therapy.

Since the focus of this book is on communication, let us examine what various clinicians might say based on their theoretical material. For example, what might Freud say to Bill, whom we met in the vignette in Chapter 1? Would he take the position of a blank screen and deal with Bill with technical neutrality? Perhaps his interpretation would be that Bill is developmentally arrested, stuck in the oral stage. How about Kernberg? I can just hear him describe Bill as an unsuitable candidate for analytic work, that he will need management skills; yet all the while Kernberg will keep in mind the analytic tools such as splitting and projective identification. How about Melanie Klein? I can imagine her calling Bill on the destructive nature of his envy and his distortions—how he is misperceiving Sara's needs as persecutory and demanding. Kohut might empathize with Bill and try his best to get Sara to serve as a better self-object for him, for her to be more of an "us," showing how pointing her finger stirs up in Bill many archaic injuries. How about Masterson? While Kohut would interpret and validate Bill's experience, Masterson would most likely confront him. "You act as though you are proud of being a borderline. But are you proud of the way you get angry and attack Sara when she reminds you of your mother?" These musings lead us to a more comprehensive literature review of some of the various theoretical approaches referred to in this book.

Talking as a Cure

About a hundred years ago, a bright but very ill young woman found that if her doctor listened to her for hours while she told him about her inner experience and her memories, the symptoms that were making her life unbearable would gradually subside. The patient recovered and went on to become the first social worker in Germany. Her doctor, Dr. Breuer, became one of the teachers of Sigmund Freud, inventor of the "talking cure"—psychoanalysis. At first the students of Freud thought that the talking cure would help all mentally ill people except those who were seriously psychotic. But over the years they found themselves dealing with some patients who were in the "borderland" described previously—people who were not psychotic but who did not respond to the talking cure in the way that therapists expected. Such patients have momentary psychosis, states of mentalization, illogic, and irrationality. Gradually, therapists began to define this "borderline" group not so much by their symptoms but by the special problems that underlay the symptoms, by the effects these people had on others, and by their stubborn resistance to therapy.

Seinfeld (1990) referred to this resistance to therapy as a "negative therapeutic reaction." In my previous publications, I refer to this as the V-spot, an area of emotional vulnerability that I liken to a nuclear reactor: One strike and it is ready to explode. With this explosion comes the loss of sensibility, the capacity to think and to make rational decisions. Everything shifts as in an earthquake: memory, perception of reality, and judgment become distorted. When the V-spot is exposed, the ego is stripped of its natural resources and its capacity to function, including the ability to mediate and contain anxiety. Instead, anxiety, which the ego does not initially view as a threat, eventually takes the form of panic when signals from the ego are circumvented. I believe this is what happened to Bill. At the moment of his outburst he was not able to think introspectively and take responsibility for not cleaning the clutter in the garage. Yet at the same time he wanted himself and his wife to be a couple in harmony and unison (could this be dialectic behavior?).

Sigmund Freud

He that has eyes to see and ears to hear may convince himself that no mortal can keep a secret. If his lips are silent, he chatters with his fingertips; betrayal oozes out of him at every pore.

—Freud quoted in *The First Dream Fragment* of "An Analysis of a Case of Hysteria" (1905)

Freud and his followers (Klein, Fairbairn, etc.) may not have known specifically about the borderline syndrome, yet they laid the groundwork by providing us with tools that today we find invaluable. Freud (1923) noted early on that there was a certain segment of patients who would behave in a peculiar fashion during analysis, and he could not understand why they would become discontent when treatment progressed. He observed that just at the pinnacle of success these patients would sabotage or destroy what they had achieved and would even go into a massive regression. Ironically, Freud was unaware that the borderline existed, let alone thinking about what to say to one. He did notice that certain patients would become defiant at any attempt at progress and react adversely to any praise or appreciation. In his famous Wolfman case (1918), Freud extrapolated that these patients had a certain proclivity for punishment (Lachkar, 2008a, 2008b).

As in the preceding case of Bill, these patients were neither insane nor mentally healthy. And they continued to puzzle psychiatrists for the next hundred years. It was in this "borderland" that society and psychiatry came to place its criminals, alcoholics, and those people who were suicidal, emotionally unstable, and behaviorally unpredictable—to separate them both from those with more clearly defined psychiatric illnesses (those, for example, whose illness we have come to call schizophrenia and manic-depressive or "bipolar" disorder) and from "normal" people at the other end of the spectrum.

Melanie Klein

Ironically, although Klein (1975) did not focus on the borderline personality, her work on primitive mental defenses has given us amazing insights into the psychological makeup of a borderline. Klein explored the relationship between mourning and primitive defenses, introducing two fundamental stages of development: the paranoid–schizoid and the depressive position. The interplay between love, envy, guilt, and reparation, to say nothing of the projective/introjective process, is fundamental not only with borderlines but with all patients. In the case of Sara and Bill, it helps us understand Sara's tendency to internalize Bill's negative projections as she identifies with them through her own internal "bad object." Klein might say that Bill is in the paranoid–schizoid position (a state of fusion with a maternal object, a non-differentiated state). Such dynamics as splitting, projection, projective identification, primitive envy, and idealization have been invaluable in providing us with insights into BPD. Unknowingly, Klein's work is a first-class version of dialectic behavioral therapy—the two stages of development continually moving back and forth between fragmentation and wholeness.

Donald Fairbairn

Why People Stay in Painful Relationships

> There can always be someone who abuses you, but there can also be a part of yourself that mistreats and abuses you.

More than anyone, Donald Fairbairn helps us understand why people/ couples (in my work even nations/groups) stay in painful, conflictual relationships, why they stay forever and loyally bonded and attached to the bad internal object. Fairbairn expanded Klein's notion of the "good and bad breast," advancing the idea that the ego does not split into two parts but into a multitude of subdivisions (rejecting object, and tantalizing, tormenting, or unavailable objects). I have extrapolated from Fairbairn's work the concept of internal/external objects and attachments to bad objects as an invaluable platform for communicating with a borderline.

Because the pain is linked to the love object, it becomes highly charged and eroticized/sexualized. This helps us understand why one will stay forever bonded to the Mother of Pain (Dutton & Painter, 1981). As bad as the pain is, it is still better than facing the abyss, the void, the black hole (Grotstein, 1981, 1987). This is what is referred to as "traumatic bonding" (Dutton & Painter, 1981; Lachkar, 1998a). Such bonding creates ambivalence, because the one who disappoints, frustrates, and offers gratuitous promises is also the who can be loving and kind.

Many borderline patients cannot feel a semblance of aliveness unless they are in a dysfunctional, destructive attachment. "Why do I stay with a woman who torments me, someone I wouldn't wish on my worst enemy? At least I feel a sense of aliveness instead of deadness." It is better to be abused than to feel nothing at all. Borderlines repeat the same drama over and over again, without ever learning from experience. The most pervasive feature is that they are more bonded to pain than pleasure and will endlessly repeat the same traumatic experience. The confusion between pain and pleasure gets carried over into adulthood. As bad as it is, it still offers a sense of aliveness. "At least I know I am alive and I exist!"

Why is it that borderlines cannot heed our "good advice?" And that even after a divorce or separation these individuals maintain a bond, albeit a destructive one? Are they crazy, perverse, or sadomasochistic? As Grotstein (1987) has illustrated, any attachment is better than no attachment. In the *Narcissistic/Borderline Couple* (Lachkar, 2004b), this "bad attachment" is

TABLE 2.1
Attachments to Bad Internal and External Objects

Negative Internal Objects	Negative External Objects
• The wronged self	• The exciting object
• The betraying self	• The unavailable object
• The abandoning self	• The withholding object
• The lost self	• The persecutory object
• The deprived self	• The scary object
• The unaware/denying self	• The sadistic object
• The rejecting self	• The avoiding object

described as coming with a feeling of loss of control and power. I refer to Fairbairn's work because it helps explain why couples stay in relationships that are guaranteed to produce trauma and deny gratification.

> *Why is it I am always falling in love with the unavailable man—married men, men who are on the rebound, the commitment phobic—and always end up getting hurt and rejected?*

Unbeknownst to Fairbairn, he has made a major contribution to our study of communication. His concept of internal/external objects helps us understand how and why people become firmly attached to a bad internal object (Table 2.1).

> *Yes, of course there can always be an external abuser or an external rejecter, but there can also be an internal abuser or rejecter. We can't control all the married men who are unfaithful to their wives, but we can help you gain control over this internal rejecter/betrayer.*

D. W. Winnicott

The Art of Playing With and Enjoying Your Borderline Patient

Donald Winnicott (1965) is another prominent figure whose unique ideas and language have enhanced and expanded the diversified field of object relations. One of his major contributions is his concept of the "false self," a self he proposed as being in constant battle with the true self or a self that cannot be found. He described this as a defense against facing disruptions or continuity within the "mother–infant matrix." He introduced varying kinds of "mothering experiences," including the "doing mother,"

TABLE 2.2
Winnicott's Different Kinds of Mothering Experiences

- The "good breast" and "bad breast" mother
- The "being and doing" mother
- The "environmental," "background" mother
- The "containing" mother
- The "rejecting," "absent," mother
- The mother of "pain"
- The "internal" mother
- The "facilitating" and "environmental" mother
- The "mirroring" mother
- The "self-object" mother
- The "idealized" mother
- The "castrating" mother
- The "introjected" mother
- The "self-hatred" mother
- The "internalized" mother
- The average expectable or "good enough mother"
- The "creative/playful" mother

Source: Lachkar, 2004b, 2008a, 2008b.

---

the "being mother," the "environmental mother," and the "containing mother" (Table 2.2). His most valuable contribution to treatment involves allowing the patient the capacity to play, dream, and fantasize in a space that is safe and conducive to creativity. The language of dialectics according to Winnicott is the movement between the false and true selves that plays out throughout a lifetime. His focus, like that of Klein, was on the importance of the early "mommy and me" relationship, which provided us with variations on the mothering experience by denoting different kinds of mothering experiences (see Table 2.2). His concept of use and misuse of the transitional object alongside a "holding/environmental mother" is at the core of his work.

Winnicott's belief was that the therapeutic environment becomes a recreation of a holding environment, a new opportunity with the therapist in the role of a "good-enough mother" who provides a good holding environment. In couples therapy, this transitional space helps partners move from states between dependency and interdependency by making use of transitional objects. What follows are two examples of the importance of Winnicott's contribution: play, and the search for the exciting object.

Importance of Play

A patient comes into the waiting room. She never sits still as she waits for her name to be called to enter the consultation room. Instead, she jumps and walks around with a gait of a school girl. With a smile on her face, she waltzes into the office. I comment that it is hard for her to sit still and wait for her appointment. "Oh, no," she says, "I want to be a ballerina like you and that is why I waltzed into your office." (This patient happens to know I take ballet and used to dance professionally.) I say that is very sweet and charming. "I'm sure Johann Strauss would have loved that; however, you have a wrong concept of ballet class. It is a very structured, formal classical setting. Dancers don't just waltz in; they have a specific protocol. They walk in and go directly to the barre to warm up. Just like here, there is a formality on how to enter."

Search for the Exciting Object

I found Fairbairn's concept of the exciting object most beneficial for a couple deliberating a divorce. This dovetails with Kernberg's work on external/internal reality (Kernberg, 1985b). The husband complained he did not find his wife sexually exciting anymore and needed to find a more exciting woman, someone who was passionately in love with him, adored him, and could not wait to be home in bed with him. The theme of looking for the exciting object eventually turned into an obsession. Finally, I said, "You are becoming obsessed with looking for excitement. Yet, you say most of the time you are bored and don't find much excitement in your life." It was at this juncture that the patient said he used to write plays but gave up because he did not have the patience and worried about failure. Well, readers, you can take it from there. As soon as he restored his "real" passion and went back to his writing, he started to feel the inner passion long ago forgotten. The external "divorce" turned out to be the "divorced" part of him. Thank you, Fairbairn and Kernberg, for saving this marriage!

Wilfred Bion

In a very profound way, the works of Bion (1961, 1962, 1967, 1977) parallel Marsha Linehan's Theory of Mentalization. For Bion, it starts with projective identification, a concept closely aligned with Linehan's "reactive responses," how a borderline reacts without cognition—a "knee-jerk" reaction. For Bion, the worst crime is to avoid truth. His biggest nemesis occurs when the patient does not think (K link). This is what he refers to as a "thought without a thinker." Bion's conception of projective identification is a form of communication, an unmentalized experience or unborn thought, also known as a "preconception." This is important because often borderlines tend to disavow their preconceptions or, shall we say, intuitive parts. Bion regards the entire purpose of treatment as twofold: first, for the therapist to make use of "preconception" as crucial to modeling how to trust and be less doubtful (borderlines tend to split off or disregard preconceptions, needs, curiosity, feelings) and second, to learn from experience without repeating the same destructive behavior time and again. So while the patient is experiencing "preconception," or intuition, it is important for the therapist to help maintain this state, the experience of "O" (Bion, 1977). In the case of Sara and Bill, Bion might say that both of them are in the state of "O," Bill being in the paranoid–schizoid position—a state of fusion with a maternal attachment that he unconsciously is trying to recreate—and Sara acting as the container for his negative and destructive projections.

James Masterson

Masterson (1981) made a major breakthrough in giving us two methods of communication: first for the narcissist and second for the borderline. He claims that narcissists are more in need of interpretation and empathy, whereas the borderline responds more to confrontation. He cites the following example of responding to a patient who expressed an incident with her mother (Masterson, 1981, p. 32). I have used this example to note the difference between the Kohut and Masterson approaches.

A young woman is hospitalized and calls to tell her mother she is in a mental hospital. The mother hears her daughter but ignores this information and makes her daughter the scapegoat, telling her that her brother is drinking again and that she, the patient, must speak to him about it. The patient reports this incident with an affect of dismay and disappointment.

Interpretation (Kohut): Even though these interactions with your mother are disappointing, you seem compelled to seek them out in order to feel good about yourself.

Confrontation (Masterson). Since these interactions disappoint you or are painful to you, why do you seek your mother out at these times? Why do you let your mother treat you this way? Masterson claims that his interpretation focuses the attention on how the daughter is destructive to herself and invites more curiosity and insight into herself, whereas Kohut's way might, on the other hand, create more resistance. In the case of Bill, I attempted to sort out the difference between his desire for intimacy and closeness and fusion. Knowing Bill, I was more inclined toward borderline organization, and keeping Masterson's concept in mind, I leaned more toward "soft" confrontation with Bill.

Heinz Kohut

Heinz Kohut's innovative approach cultivated a new theory of self-psychology designed mainly for those with narcissistic personalities. He believed that over time he could transform or convert those patients who exhibit borderline personalities into "analyzable narcissists." Although Kohut brought us the gift of empathy, he also understood the concept of containment, or what he refers to as "stand the heat." His approach included supportive interventions, empathy, validation, and understanding the perceptions of others, as well as assuming that these perceptions are not to be challenged. Kernberg, on the other hand, avoided supportive approaches and felt they undermined the work within the transference/countertransference modality. Kernberg had a more severe method to confront the patient's distortions, miscommunications, exaggerations, and out-of-context material, focusing particularly on the patient's negativity and disparaging remarks about others and making him/her aware of the split-off aspects in order to allow integration to occur. Kohut's approach, although certainly important, is less suited to treat the more severe borderline patients. In fact, for many borderline patients empathy can be misunderstood as weakness. Basically, Kohut's theory was not inclined to deal with aggression and the patient's unleashed rage.

Otto Kernberg

Kernberg has done the most comprehensive work in the literature on the borderline personality. In conceptualizing the borderline, he has written extensively about various kinds of borderlines and their overlap. More important, he was one of the first to recognize that classical analysis was not effective with borderline patients and that they needed a more "hands-on" approach—what he refers to as the "here and now." He focused on educating patients to regulate their moods by recognizing the triggers that cause them. This, he claims, helps them to connect actions with thoughts and feelings in both self and other. Furthermore, he recognizes the need for antidepressant and mood-stabilizing drugs to help with affect regulation. Despite all the new approaches, his work remains fundamental to current psychoanalytic thinking regarding the borderline patient. Stepping away from the classical approach—the position of neutrality and of waiting for the patient to come up with a thought, an idea, an association—Kernberg felt the therapist should be more interactive and "use as many words as necessary" to help the patient in the moment of thoughtlessness/thinklessness or unmentalization (Kobrin, 2010, personal communication).

Marsha Linehan

This book would not be complete without the inclusion of Marsha Linehan's work on Dialectical Behavior Therapy (DBT). It is based on a biosocial theory of borderline personality disorder as a consequence of an emotionally vulnerable individual growing up within a particular set of environmental circumstances that she refers to as the "invalidating environment." Linehan reinforces the notion that the "validating," nonjudgmental environment offers an opportunity to regulate affect and self-soothe. Her concepts involve situations in which the personal experiences and responses of the growing child are disqualified or "invalidated" by the significant others in his/her life. She views dialectic treatment as a balance between acceptance and change. First she emphasizes the importance of accepting the invalidating environment: for example, if a child is hungry and the mother says, "That is impossible because you just ate." Or the child is upset and the mother says, "You have nothing to be upset about." In the case of Bill and Sara, DBT therapy would accept Bill's position as the need to be an "us," without addressing the confusion between "us-ness" and closeness.

DBT was devised by Marsha Linehan at the University of Washington in Seattle specifically to treat borderline personality disorders in a way that is optimistic and preserves the morale of the therapist. Linehan refers to borderlines as "emotionally vulnerable" people whose autonomic nervous system reacts excessively to relatively low levels of stress and takes longer than normal to return to baseline once the stress is removed. She proposes that this is the consequence of a biological diathesis.

In the last 25 years Dialectic Behavioral Therapy has become increasingly popular and respected, particularly as a method for minimizing the tendency among BPD patients to make suicide gestures or attempts or to indulge in other forms of self-harm. This treatment approach includes one individual session per week with a therapist, along with a weekly group session oriented toward skills training. DBT involves continuous validation and acceptance of the patient's perception as an important part of the healing process, reassuring the patient that the negative experiences really did happen (abuse, betrayal, punishment). Linehan works with two poles: what the patient feels did happen and what really happened. I believe this approach is closely akin to Kohut's concept of empathy and mirroring of the patient's subjective experience. I take the concept a step further and challenge the idea of "acceptance." I accept the patient's true self but not the patient's defenses.

Although DBT integrates transference, it applies a cognitive approach rather than a transference-focused psychotherapy. Borderline patients are difficult to treat, particularly when suicidal and parasuicidal behaviors are prominent. Linehan also notes that borderlines are particularly challenged by the "invalidating environment," especially those who always look externally for validation. This creates psychic confusion that causes erratic behavior; movements oscillate between opposite poles, resulting in "emotional deregulation" that combines in a transactional manner with the invalidating environment to produce the typical symptoms of borderline personality disorder.

Mentalization-Based Therapy

Mentalization-Based Therapy (MBT) is an alternative treatment method specifically designed to help patients with borderline personality separate their inner thoughts from outer reality. Anthony Bateman and Peter Fonagy developed the theory of mentalization within the context of an attachment relationship. They claim that patients whose inner lives are chaotic and disorganized have a harder time thinking clearly, or "mentalizing." The theory behind MBT is that we develop the capacity to mentalize within the context of an attachment relationship and in an environment that fosters it. Bateman and Fonagy argue that people with BPD have difficulty mentalizing, and that it is particularly hard for them to recognize internal states and motivations, especially in interpersonal and intimate situations. People with BPD have a certain vulnerability about getting into intense relationships, then end up being so overwhelmed emotionally that they cannot think clearly.

MBT differs from DBT in that it tackles the conflict through interpretation, by helping the patient explore whether he/she is open to alternative possibilities. I am reminded of the patient who assumed I was not interested in what she had to say because I turned my head away. By assuring her that I was so interested in her comment that I needed to think about how to respond to it, I allowed her to explore another possibility for my actions.

In the case of Sara and Bill, Bill is not aware of his confused mental state. He thinks he is asking for closeness and intimacy, but he is really enacting a fantasy of closeness, a fusion with a maternal object long ago abandoned (the early archaic injury or V-spot). The fusion in this instance is the unmentalized experience. For example, Sara tells Bill to stop being so possessive and controlling. Bill yells back, "But this is the way I am, and that is who I am!" The therapist addresses Bill's confusion this way: "Bill, this is not who you are. You are basically a very independent, high-functioning professional. When you think you are demanding closeness or 'togetherness,' you are really asking to fuse with Sara—an enactment of what you needed with your mother. You would like to have a healthy relationship with your wife, but first we have to help you understand the difference between closeness and fusion." The difference between the analytic approach and the DBT approach would be that the DBT therapist would accept Bill's desire for "closeness" as a given and not go into the more primitive defenses, the urge to fuse with a maternal object.

Since mentalization-based therapy focuses closely on observation, I find it more liberating than DBT because it invites the therapist into the patient's experience. This is essential for emotionally overwhelmed borderlines, who need to understand how people can misperceive their thoughts. This is why I believe a psychodynamic approach makes a perfect bedfellow for BPD patients. The borderline has thoughts that are viewed as dangerous and toxic—thoughts that are the equivalent of an emotional virus, thoughts not processed or put into a language suitable for thinking—Bion's "thoughts without a thinker." Although it is not within the scope of this book, we could extend this concept to gender differences. Women, the bearers of children, are by nature able to pick up an infant's nonverbal language (screams and cries), whereas men would find them terrifying (of course, there are always exceptions). In shame cultures, many man have not been able to process these unmentalized cries, and the child is left with feelings of shame to ward off neglected internal voices.

A. J. Mahari

In *The Borderline Dance and the Non-Borderlines' Dilemma* (2009), Mahari shares her experience as a survivor of sexual abuse and her recovery from borderline personality disorder. She talks about survival for the borderline and the nonborderline's dilemma in the relationship. She is one of the few authors who actually attempts to show the nonborderline partner how to communicate. She states that when one is in a relationship with a borderline, one must have a plan of action and consistently stick to it. When one finally decides to try a new approach to communicate with the borderline, she suggests speaking only of one's own experience and refraining from in any way addressing the borderline's behavior. This will come across as an attack. She states that the nonborderline partner must be direct, honest, fair, and not overly concerned with how the borderline will react. I gather that she is saying not to get caught in the borderline's projective identification. "I feel terrified; therefore I will terrify you." Before we communicate with a borderline, Mahari suggests that we first understand how the borderline sets him/herself up to reexperience and reenact that which feels familiar, no matter how painful it might be (betrayal/abandonment).

The Borderline Dilemma

A. J. Mahari and Marsha Linehan share similar concerns regarding the borderline dilemma. This syndrome is as perplexing for therapists as it is for nonborderlines. The ego disturbances and poor ego functioning compounded by surrounding primitive defenses prevent them from maintaining healthy object relations. In a few simple words, "We are damned if we do and damned if we don't." In the language of dialectics, it underscores the splitting mechanism as it attacks the ego's ability to function, to observe, to think, to judge, and to perceive. Mrs. W. insisted that it would help if she could call a few times a day to hear my voice. We agreed until finally it got so out of hand that the phone was ringing nonstop, to say nothing about the clicking sounds from calls waiting. When I asked Mrs. W. to limit her calls she became enraged, accusing me of depriving her and going back on my word. If I tell her the calls are excessive, she will argue they are not excessive and then we get into a battle. If I tell her they are intrusive, she will complain that my contacts with others are more important than with her. If I overlook the above, I will feel invaded. Instead, I let her know that her need to call was an indication that she needed more than a once-a-week psychotherapy session and that her need for contact was healthy. Thus, instead of getting into a battle with Mrs. W., which was certainly easy to do, I invited her to add an extra session. Another challenge with Mrs. W. occurs at the end of the session. I find myself saying endless good-byes but to no avail. If I say good-bye and close the door, I will be besieged with endless calls for throwing her out. If I wait at the door for her to leave, I am besieged with endless doorknob forget-me-nots. "Oh, just once more thing! Oh, I forget to tell you." The final dilemma with Mrs. W. are the hugs. If I do not hug her, I am cold and aloof like her mother. If I do hug her, I am overstepping my therapeutic boundaries. Wherever I turn with Mrs. W. I am in a double bind. What follows are some examples of how to respond, integrating the following themes:

The Insatiable Self	Therapist as the Depriver
The Baby Self	Therapist as the Withholder
	(nonfeeding mother)
The Rejected Self	Therapist as the Rejecter

- In response to the endless telephone calls, I address the insatiable, deprived baby part, which believes that after I give permission I betray her.
- In response to the end-of-session dilemma, I address the unconscious part that sets herself up for rejection. "You know the session ends at a certain time, so you set me up to throw you out. I never want to do that. I always like to say a cordial good-bye to you."
- In response to the accusation of being a betrayer, I answer, "I didn't betray you. I changed my mind. You and I are not stuck here; we have options."
- To address the "hugs," I tell her, "It's not that I don't want to hug you. In fact there are times I do. But you're only thinking about rejection, and then you're not available to see that I am trying to maintain a healthy professional, ethical, and safe environment for both of us (ego dysfunctionality).

Throughout the treatment the therapist actually should pay less attention to the behaviors and actions than to the themes, to which he or she should pay very acute attention. Stay with the covert communication. Listen to the words, like the thematic motif in music or poetry. Stay with the feelings, the here and

TABLE 2.3
Ego Functions

Type	Description
Reality testing	Refers to the ego's capacity to distinguish what occurs in one's own mind and what occurs in the external world, as well as the ability to perceive outer stimuli accurately. When the ego is flooded or overwhelmed, it is more susceptible to a distorted sense of reality.
Impulse control	The inability to delay instant gratification and contain/manage internal aggressive and/or libidinal forces such as promiscuity, drugs, alcoholism, binge eating, road rage. Poor tolerance for frustration. "The jumpy little girl inside can't wait. She has to do it right now!"
Affect regulation	The ability to modify/control feelings without being overwhelmed.
Judgment	The capacity to make rational/reasonable decisions based on reality, not wishes or fantasy. This includes the ability to anticipate and evaluate possible consequences of one's actions and act appropriately.
Interpersonal relations and object relations	On the surface, borderlines seem to relate well to others. Ego fragmentation occurs when the relationship deepens or the capacity for intimacy reaches its peak. Instead of embracing the intimacy, the tendency is to avoid the feelings of vulnerability and to attack the object. Partners of borderlines get very confused about the vacillation between intense dependency, superficiality, and longing for love.
Thought process	The ability to have logical, coherent thoughts and the capacity for abstract thinking as opposed to the concrete (black and white). Severe problems in conceptual thinking are frequently associated with schizophrenia and other severe mental disorders.
Primitive ego defenses/psychodynamics	Defenses are often an unconscious attempt to cover or protect the self from some internal threat. These include splitting, projection, projective identification, omnipotent denial, idealization, and devaluation. Borderlines are dominated by issues of abandonment, betrayal, persecutory anxiety, emptiness, suspiciousness, paranoia, impulsivity, mistrust, distorted thought processes. They have difficulty regulating emotions.

Type	Description
	TABLE 2.3 (CONTINUED) **Ego Functions**
Identity diffusion	Borderlines are very polarized (nonintegrated self), and often see the world as all good or all bad. If they internalize the object mother as all bad, they will project the bad mother into people they meet and interact with. They are unable to balance the negative with the positive. "My mother was bad and abusive; therefore, the teacher is bad when she gives me a bad grade." Borderlines exhibit identity disturbance and a markedly and persistently unstable self-image or sense of self. Because of the lack of a clear identity, borderlines often feel a black hole or void they are constantly seeking to fill. Often they will resort to a negative identity rather than none at all. "I'm a borderline!"
Synthesis	The synthetic function of the ego is the capacity to organize and unify the various functions within the personality, enabling the person to think and act coherently. A married woman may want to divorce her husband but then realizes that with three small children, it may not be a wise move.

the now, and the projections (the invasion, the betrayal, the depriver). Swallow them, take them in, and transform them into a more palatable form.

The Ego and Its Dysfunctionality

The ego is not the master in its own house.

—Sigmund Freud (1923)

What is an ego? It is a very slippery term, and even the most well-seasoned analysts sometimes lose sight of the ego's importance and the area of the psyche it governs. The ego is part of an intrapsychic system responsible for functioning (thinking, reality testing, and judgment). It is the mediator between the id and superego. The function of the ego is to observe the external world, preserving a true picture by eliminating memory traces left by early impressions and perceptions. Most people think the ego is not user-friendly, because they spend a good part of their lives trying to avoid truth and reality.

Basically, the ego can be our best friend because it helps us to observe our self and our own behavior. Why is the ego important in assessing the borderline? People are often shocked and surprised at the outrageous behavior of the borderline. "Isn't she aware of how she talks nonstop? Doesn't she see how she gets on people's nerves always complaining about her aches and pains?" What makes a borderline think he or she has a right to attack, yell, scream, lose control, lie, or sabotage? Why do we see things that borderlines do not see? Because of ego deficiency, borderlines are lacking in introspection and do not have the regulatory mechanism of the observing ego to guide them. This makes their behavior visually transparent to others, like the parable of the Emperor's New Clothes. Everyone could see he was naked except the Emperor himself. Table 2.3 contains ego functions to look for in sessions when assessing the borderline.

In the next chapter we embark on our exploration of the eight types of borderlines and the ways to best communicate with each type. Chapter 3 examines the Pathological Borderline, the first—and the least harmful—of the eight borderline typologies outlined in this book.

3

The Pathological Borderline

The pathological borderline is the least toxic of all the borderlines described in this book. Although there is a great deal of variance among pathological borderlines—mainly in their defense mechanisms, behaviors, and psychodynamics—differentiating between different kinds of borderlines, even within a specific category, is not an easy task. In my assessment, pathological borderlines are basically confused. They inhabit a chaotic internal world, cannot sort out or organize the data of experience, and basically are not as unintentionally cruel and sadistic as their malignant borderline brothers. As we saw in the case of Tom in Chapter 1—a stellar example of a pathological borderline—he is not intentionally destructive or malicious, although his behaviors can exhaust and exasperate those around him. Typically, pathological borderlines are not physically abusive, suicidal, harmful, or destructive to themselves or others. Instead, they operate on a more primitive level of functioning, using defense mechanisms such as delusions, distortions, splitting, magical thinking, omnipotent denial, and projective identification. Many of these defenses are inextricably linked to splitting, the epicenter that creates confusion and chaos. "Just last week you were telling me how thrilled you were to find a therapist like me, and now you are telling me you are very angry with me!" I am reminded of a patient who had a dream that illustrates this point.

> *I dreamt that I was digging a hole at an archeological site where I found a gold treasure. I suddenly realized it was you, my therapist. When I held it up it turned into a piece of dirt. I then threw it into the trash.*

What Makes the Pathological Borderline So Taxing?

Is it the way they walk into the consult room with a smirk on their face? Is it the way they stare at you as if they can see through your impermeable membrane? Is it the way they look at you suspiciously when you ask a rather simple question or comment? Is it the way they make you feel you better watch your every word or step? Is it the way they sit in silence with a blank stare as if you do not exist? Is it the long silences awaiting a response? Is it the way they look at you as if they know something you do not know? Is it their intrusiveness and desire to know everything about you, looking around the office for the slightest change in environment or your appearance? ("Oh, you colored your hair. You lost weight. Is that new?") Is it the fear they put into you when they ask if you remember something they said and you have forgotten? How about the cancellation the day before, the long wait for the call to reschedule, and the accusation of not being "understanding" if you charge for the appointment? How about the eyes? The scary eyes? The blank, staring, restless, invasive, pleading, or piercing eyes? How about when you interrupt them to say something and they go into an emotional outburst? "I was talking. Will you let me finish! You are always interrupting me!" When this occurs, I might respond as follows.

> *Yes, I do intervene when I see you are going into another direction, and I know how much time means to you. I did not mean to be rude in any way.*

This particular patient treats me with contempt, as if I am her greatest enemy, then after her session will typically call several times to apologize. This is example of the dialectic interaction, how she blames me for forgetting what she was about to say, as if I am the one who prevents her from remembering what is on her mind. This follows with an endless effort to reassure her after each sentence that she is being heard. We go round and round until finally I am able to connect to her "unheard child" by letting her know how she was treating me like her mother treated her, castigating me as her mother did with her. "I am the child and you are my critical, intrusive, disruptive mommy, the 'real' intrusive voiceover." My response relieved and enabled her to look at our object relational bond.

What follows is another example of this character formation, and the stresses and strain the pathologic borderline puts on the therapist. I recall my experience with Ms. X, a 49-year-old woman who had been in treatment two times weekly for the past nine years. Although she was playful in a kind of "cutesy" way, what she found "cutesy" I found obnoxious. I repeatedly asked myself why it was that she could not see nor observe her own process. Does she not see how her behavior turns off others, given her inappropriate waiting room behavior? Does she not see that the very closeness and intimacy she craves is that which she destroys? I remind myself that she lacks the observing ego, and therefore I have to become her observer. I remember cringing every time I enter the waiting room to invite her in. Instead of sitting quietly reading a magazine or just waiting patiently for her session, she would jump around the room, look around, and sing loudly (sometimes I could hear singing faintly through the walls of the consult room). "Oh, can I borrow this magazine? Is this plant new? What happened to the painting that used to be here?" With each agonizing step into the consultation room, I would gesture her to have a seat. Instead, she would walk around the office and examine each artifact like an entomologist, as if she were seeing them for the first time. "Oh, I think that picture is crooked! Do you mind if I straighten it?" For a while I gave her a free reign, and later explored with her how she comes into my office like a child going into a kindergarten class (jumpy, happy, playful). Her association was surprisingly insightful and quite on the mark. She recalled a childhood as the eldest of four siblings, and having to be the caretaker for her mother as well as her younger siblings. Feeling her childhood was usurped, this was her time to play, be silly, have fun, and act out. In Winnicottian terms, we could refer to this as her transforming me into the role of the playful mommy, allowing her the transitional space to reenact her drama.

Dancing With the Pathological Borderline

In my earlier works, I refer to the "dance of the couple," interactions that go round and round without ever reaching any conflict resolution. This "dance" was more clearly defined in *The Narcissistic/Borderline Couple* (Lachkar, 1992, 2004b) and illustrates what happens when a narcissist and a borderline get together, and how through the introjective/projective process each one stirs up some unconscious, undeveloped part in the other. In psychological terms this is known as the early archaic injury, or what I refer to as the vulnerable spot (the "V-spot"). Here is an example of dancing with a pathological borderline and what happens when the narcissist tries to obliterate the borderline's needs. Note how the borderline's endless state of victimization, blame/shame/attacking defenses evoke guilt in the narcissist, and how the rejecting self-absorbed narcissist evokes feelings of worthlessness, deprivation, and abandonment in the borderline. "The only way I can get my narcissistic husband to listen to me is when I am sick, in a crisis, or threaten suicide. He makes me feel like my needs are bad and dangerous, so I always have to go into a crisis. It becomes a no-win situation, because then I become a victim, a state which he absolutely deplores." Thus it becomes a dance between guilt and shame, shame for the borderline to have needs, and guilt for the narcissist who is attacked for not being perfect. The "dance" remains a dialectic study, with movements back and forth between the inner psychic world and the outer reality.

The case of Tom in Chapter 1 describes a type of borderline who is not intentionally sadistic or cruel, but whose behaviors and chaotic state can frustrate and exhaust the therapist's empathy. The therapist uses the Language of Dialectics to concentrate on the back-and-forth, rondo-like movement between the validating and invalidating environment. The challenge is to move away from the surface-externalized events to the patient's internal ones and zero in on the pathological borderline's own unique way of experiencing these dynamics. To continue with the "dance," the various types of borderlines have their own character formation and own unique way of projecting, especially shame. In communicating with borderlines, it is important for the therapist to note how each type experiences these various dynamics and to be aware of their qualitative differences in order to shape an appropriate and fitting communication.

For example, the way an obsessive–compulsive borderline experiences shame may be entirely different from the way a pathological borderline experiences shame. The obsessive–compulsive may try to ward off shame by an excessive obsession with cleaning, wiping, filing, meticulously inspecting— needing to be reassured again and again in order to ward off a fantasized "dirty" internal world where emotions, needs, feelings, dependency are felt to be filthy and disgusting: "those little creepy, crawling things inside of me!" I am reminded of a patient who, when referring to needs, would respond, "What? And open a can of worms?" In contrast, the pathological borderline does not feel his or her needs are dirty or disgusting, but will feel persecuted and suffocated by them. "Why should I tell you what I need and open myself up for rejection?"

This is in contrast to the malignant borderline who is more sadistic and destructive in nature and who terrorizes their objects. "I saw it coming. I saw terror in his eyes. Just then he took his fist and bashed it through the wall!"

Many borderlines mask their "needy" selves to avoid contact with normal and healthy dependency needs. Shame is like a virus that invades and infects the psyche. This dynamic is typical especially in "shame/honor" cultures, in which one is taught to avoid looking someone in the eye as a cultural emollient to being shamed (Kobrin, 2010, personal communication). Shame is more pronounced than guilt, and occurs in the paranoid–schizoid position as a matter between the person, the group, or society.

Because the borderline is more dominated by shame than guilt, it is noteworthy that many borderlines lack the normal superego functions and operate from the primitive superego in accordance with Melanie Klein's (1957) paranoid–schizoid position,

Pathological Borderlines and the Negative Reactions They Trigger in Others

Dancing with a pathological borderline is not an easy task, because their projections stir up many unconscious feelings and fantasies in others around them, especially those who have the proclivity to identify with the negative projections and behaviors of the borderline. Among the many anxieties and primitive defenses pathological borderlines evoke in those with whom they interact are shame, guilt, envy, jealousy, and feelings of nonexistence. The person functioning on a higher level may not be as affected by the negativity of the pathological borderline as those more inclined toward certain emotional vulnerabilities. The following case is an example of how we "dance" with a borderline.

Case of Laura and Benny, the Invisible Husband

Laura, a mother of three children who is married to a pathological borderline, complains that whenever she disciplines her children, her husband, Benny, sits around staring at the wall as if she were an invisible object. He offers no support. At other times, just at the high point of her frustration, he withdraws to the bedroom and watches TV. Laura is basically a high-functioning woman with a great deal of integrity, but regardless would lose it when her husband disassociated from any kind of family involvement or confrontation.

I agreed to consult with Benny and was immediately able to diagnose and evaluate his borderline condition. He fit the pattern of patients who suffer from early loss and abandonment. In this case it was mainly the death of Benny's father at an early age. When asked why he refused to participate in the discipline of his children, he was surprisingly very honest and open. This led to the assessment of his identity confusion, how—not having a father to identify with—he never learned how to be a father, let alone a husband, and still feels as though he is a little boy in his mother's home. When we met in the next conjoint session with Laura, it was helpful and reassuring that Benny was not purposely ignoring her or devaluing her as a mother or wife, although developmentally he was not yet able to fit the "job" description of husband and father. After identifying the dilemma, Benny agreed to continue working on his issues around identification. Some of the work we did went as follows:

> *Benny, I totally understand your dilemma, and certainly you don't want to come across as a phony or being someone you're not. However, in reality, whether we feel the role or not we all have to play the roles bestowed upon us. I have to play my role as a therapist, and when at home I have to play a different one. For now, it may seem kind of false, but meanwhile, I will help you by giving you some tools, techniques, and some specific communication methods to help you until it begins to feel more natural.*

Case of Julie and Jerry

Julie, the pathological borderline in this relationship, meets at least six of the DSM-IV criteria for borderline personality disorder (BPD), including an unstable ability to maintain an intimate relationship characterized by out-of-control and inappropriate behavior. It is also notable that she exhibits poor reality testing, fluctuations in identity, feelings of nonexistence, emptiness, and frantic attempts to avoid abandonment.

In the conjoint sessions with Jerry, all Julie would hear from him was abandonment, abandonment, and abandonment. Unable to monitor and observe her own behavior, how she stirred up rage and resentment in her husband, she was unable to understand how her violent outbursts of screaming and yelling, her fits of rage that included throwing pots and pans and dishes led her partner to continually threaten her with divorce. She was unable to observe that her husband would throw up his hands in absolute frustration. "Ok, Julie, it's over. Let's get a divorce." She was also unable to recognize that Jerry's frustration and threats of divorce were just his way of blowing off steam. Julie took his threats of divorce literally, even though the reality was that he had been saying this for the past 12 years.

During conjoint treatments, Julie would enter the room with her husband, walk pompously in front of him, and sneer at me as if I were her worst enemy. She frequently would bring a sandwich, often a rather redolent tuna sandwich, and would ask if it was okay for her to eat it since she was starving. I went with that. My response was to go into what Linehan refers to as acceptance mode and dare not remind her that there was a sign in the waiting room that said there was no food allowed. As we proceeded, I tried to console Julie by letting her know that her husband's threats of divorce seemingly were not seen as realistic, thinking that this would result in a soothing reaction. Instead, she attacked me for invalidating her reality of the threat. This put me in a position not only of do I dare take her food away but do I dare take her reality away.

This case is a very good example of relating to internal and external objects. As our work proceeded, I was able to show Julie how there can be an external abandoner but that there can also be a part of her that abandons or threatens her. "This internal threat is far more frightening than the outer one. Your first reaction is that you are going to be abandoned and rejected. This one you can control by recognizing that these are not real threats but merely expressions of Jerry's frustration."

The Wedding and the Borderline Mother

Whether it be an intimate partner, a business associate, a family member, a hairdresser, or caretaker, pathological borderlines stir up many anxieties in those around them. One does not have to be a clinician to understand the conflicts that arise during such occasions as weddings, birthdays, Bar Mitzvahs, Valentine's Day, communions, anniversaries, and of course the most conflicting of all—mediation and divorce. Obviously, these highly charged events, whether they bring joy and happiness or pain and frustration, can be stressful for anyone, but especially those inclined toward certain emotional vulnerabilities.

Lisa was so excited when her very prominent banker fiancé proposed, and then immediately scheduled a wedding with 300 guests at one of the most prestigious hotels around. Lisa couldn't wait to tell her borderline mother, or the "Mother of Pain," that she was finally engaged. To this day, she recalls the shock and disappointment when she called her mother to announce her engagement. She was met with a perfunctory, "Oh, that's nice. When is the wedding?" "Mom," she says, "I thought you would be thrilled!" "Yes, of course I am!" But she couldn't fool Lisa. Lisa knew that voice all too well. It was a voice of shame, envy, and jealousy—as if to say, "How come you get all this happiness, and I am living all alone without a husband or anyone to help support me!" This was only the beginning of Lisa's saga. Her mother did everything she could to sabotage the wedding plans and the wedding. Starting with the engagement party, she insisted she would come only if her ex-husband was not invited, in spite of the advice of the wedding planner who emphatically said it went against protocol and was unacceptable. The borderline mother did attend the engagement party, but came in drunk and dressed very inappropriately. Her appalling behavior did not end there. It was followed by one episode after another, a barrage of constant sabotage.

In subsequent therapy sessions, Lisa and I discussed her mother's being a pathological borderline personality fraught with envy, shame, and jealousy. The patient was advised to set very strong limits and boundaries on her relationship with her mother, and to enlist the support of other family members to carry these out. There was to be no contact until the mother agreed to get some therapeutic help (individual and/or family therapy).

Bonding With Pain

In many of my earlier contributions, I discuss a common syndrome—how the borderline bonds with his objects through pain. As bad as the pain is, it is still "better" than the emptiness the borderline often experiences. What follow are examples of typical ways in which the pathological borderline bonds with the "Mother of Pain" (Dutton & Painter, 1981). "When I cut or mutilate myself it hurts, but at least I know I am alive!" This also is applicable for addictive behaviors (alcohol, drugs, sex addiction, gambling).

- People who have had traumatic experiences are programmed to bond with a painful internal object that is familiar.
- It is better to bond in pain than to have to face the void, black hole, or emptiness.
- Pain stirs up an amalgam of unresolved infantile issues.
- Pain becomes highly eroticized or sexualized.
- Pain is familiar (familiar internal bad object).
- Pain is confusing: the lover who can be cruel and sadistic can also be loving and kind.
- Pain is linked to the internal part of oneself that wants to destroy/rid the self of internal and external abusers.
- Bonding through psychosomatic illness.

Mediation

Mediators are very accustomed to working with difficult problems and disputes and with upset divorcing and divorced parents. There are, however, some parents who continually sabotage the possibility of ever reaching an agreement or of getting things settled. It is often both fascinating and frustrating to observe the way these parents see the other parent as causing all the problems. Both parents appear blind to how they themselves made the situation worse and how they each sabotage their own children. (Lachkar, 1986)

The saddest part about these intensely emotional, non-ending parental conflicts is the way their children are hopelessly trapped in the middle. (Bienenfeld, 1986, pp. 39–42)

How the borderline stays bonded to the pain is often exemplified during the time of divorce or court mediation. In an article I wrote in the *Conciliation Court Review* (1986), "Narcissistic/Borderline Couples: Implications for Mediation. Courts Beware of the Borderline," reference was made to certain types of characterological personality disorders, including borderlines and narcissists who keep the court system tied up endlessly without ever reaching a conflict resolution. The irony that puzzled me was that even when they got what they wanted, they did not really want it. They remained angry, endlessly trying to get revenge, retaliate, get even with the partner who betrayed them. What most court officials do not understand is that the pathological borderline never separated from mother's body. They will sacrifice their lives, their children, their finances, do anything to get back at the world. Retaliation becomes a more pervasive force than life itself—an emotional jihad!

In contrast to the pathological borderline—the least toxic of the borderline personalities—the malignant borderline, the subject of the next chapter, is the most toxic type.

4

The Malignant Borderline

I found your name on your Web site as someone who could possibly recommend a therapist to me in the South Carolina area. I find myself over and over again with men who are abusive. Currently, I am trying to end an emotional affair of six years with a borderline. He is an alcoholic and, when over the top, he beats me, threatens me, and tells me I am nothing but a piece of shit. I am a highly functioning woman—a counselor myself with a master's degree. Pathetic, isn't it? Ending this relationship has made me suicidal at times. Do you know of any referrals in this area or at least someone close by I can work with? Can you please help me?

It is impossible to discuss malignant borderlines without taking into account both their libidinal and aggressive aspirations and their link to a sadistic superego. Because most of the focus has been placed on malignant narcissists and very little on malignant borderlines (Kernberg, 1992; Vaknin, 2007), my objective is to provide a descriptive account relevant for diagnostic treatment and communication consideration.

The malignant borderline personality has many similarities with the malignant narcissist. Both are characterized by difficulties in maintaining intimacy and defects in superego functioning. However, the malignant borderline is distinguished by their willingness to resort to brutal cruelty, both emotional and physical (Vaknin, 2007). Lawson (2000) notes that children who are victims of severe abuse grow up with the expectation of being hurt. Kernberg (1985a) expands this concept further by referencing serial killers, noting that the fear of rejection or intimacy can be so overpowering that the only way some can relate is by comparing themselves to dead victims or even talking to decapitated heads; others retaliate against society. A good example of this is Eric Harris and Dylan Klebold, who were two high school seniors at Columbine High School. On April 20, 1999, they massacred and killed 12 students at their Colorado school. In an unprecedented situation, they also injured 21 other students, before they committed suicide. Both took pleasure in taunting their victims, who writhed in pain until Harris and Klebold finished them off.

Even though Kernberg does refer to serial killers as malignant narcissists, he confirms that the secondary personality is a primarily aggressive one (sadistic), with secondary antisocial and paranoid features. Because of the degree of cruelty, we might say the malignant borderline is the pathological borderline's id. Cullen's (2009) account of Harris's diagnosis includes an assessment of primarily aggressive (sadistic) personality with secondary antisocial, narcissistic, and paranoid features. Cullen concludes that this personality configuration is more consistent with psychopathy than narcissism.

In saying that Harris, one of the Columbine killers, had secondary *antisocial* features, I acknowledge that he was a psychopath. However, it is clear that I view him as primarily sadistic. In this regard, I should note that the absence of sadistic personality disorder from the standard psychiatric nomenclature forces diagnosticians to combine sadistic personality and psychopathy (or sociopathy) into a single entity, namely antisocial personality disorder. For example, in Cullen's article, it is clear that Hare's Psychopath Checklist encompasses both antisocial and sadistic traits. I address the antisocial personality disorder as a crossover with the sadistic personality—someone who is cruel, whose intent is to inflict pain, and who gets a pervasive sense of gratification from their torturous acts (both emotional and physical). Borderline gratification ranges from watching the victim squirm, rejoicing in the pain that he/she inflicts, identifying with the pain, or more commonly gaining a sense of power, control, to domination over their victims. "Now you are the needy one, and I am in power!"

In the attempt to understand this type of pathology, suitable deference must be shown to Melanie Klein and her innovative concept of projective identification. In the borderline, we see projective identification in full bloom. "Now I will deprive you the way I was deprived, and you will know what it feels like." According to Klein (1957), this kind of abuse originates in early infancy, linked to the "bad-breast mother," who is seen not as the feeding breast but as the devouring and depriving one. Because this source of comfort and safety is so needed, it also becomes the source of envious attack and therefore must be destroyed. Instead of growing up believing the world is a healthy benevolent place, the child's life is filled with despair, doom, and neglect. Klein's concepts intimate that the deprived child then finds suffering in others compatible with his own: "Let 'em squirm. I'll cut out your baby from your womb as my mother cut me from her breast!"

The line between pathological and malignant borderlines is a bit blurred, but in terms of communication these distinctions are important. Let us take, for example, the issue of deprivation to amplify these differences.

> *Pathological Borderline* (disavowal of the person's importance or existence): "You did not show up for your son's birthday party because you don't feel your presence matters or that you exist as a father—just as your father didn't exist in your life."

> *Malignant Borderline* (a displacement of rage and the intent to inflict pain). "You did not show up for your son's birthday party and denied him joy and happiness because you were deprived as a child. So why should you let him have pleasure?"

In the first example, the language of dialectics might be as follows:

> *So, because you don't feel like a father, you don't think your presence is important. You did not show up at your son's birthday party. But in reality you are a father, and your presence is vital.*

In the second example, the language of dialectics might be as follows:

> *So, it is hard to give your child pleasure because you want him to know how deprived you were as a child. But in reality giving him pleasure in no way disavows your suffering or the cruelty and neglect you had to endure.*

Traits and Characteristics of the Malignant Borderline

- Humiliates and demeans people, including children and spouses, in the presence of others.
- As parent, spouse, boss, or authority figure, creates rules and demands that are impossible to fulfill.
- Dispenses harsh, unwarranted disciplinary measures designed to create fear and control.
- Lies to create confusion in order to destroy the will and perception of the other person.
- Cannot tolerate facing responsibility for any wrongdoings.

- Is cruel to children, animals, gays, or people of different racial backgrounds.
- Lies and cheats for the purpose of inflicting pain or to achieve control at any cost.
- Threatens other people to get them to bend to his/her will by terrorizing and intimidating them.
- Restricts independent thinking and accuses others of being wrong or crazy if they do not comply—for example, "If you dare call the police or get a restraining order against me, I will cut you off completely, and you will have no money or anything. So watch your step."
- Everyone under his control must obey and never question or challenge his authority.
- Considers that to disobey is to be disloyal.
- Regards work as everything; if the family has needs, they will have to sacrifice as he or she had to.

Because of their lack of object constancy, as well as their mood swings, paranoia, and unresolved oedipal conflicts, borderlines destroy and sabotage. Unlike the narcissist who strives for success and seeks self-objects to achieve that aspiration, the borderline will destroy self-objects. This is the difference between such criminals as Bernie Madoff, Charles Manson, and Susan Atkins.

On May 19, 2009, Bernard Madoff, also known as the Ponzi Prince, was accused of severe embezzlement, with 11 felony counts that included securities fraud, mail fraud, money laundering, and perjury. He was sentenced to 150 years in prison. Manson family member Susan Atkins was given a life sentence when she was convicted of killing and stabbing Sharon Tate 16 times. Even when Tate, pregnant at the time, begged for her baby's life, Atkins replied that she had no mercy on her. Obviously, most of us in clinical practice do not have the opportunity to treat such high-profile criminals or their families. However, the fantasy analysis that follows shows how borderline communication techniques and distinctions might be applicable if such a scenario did occur in your consultation room. It also exemplifies the treatment approach that would be best suited to treating a shocked, demoralized spouse or family member.

Fantasy Analysis With Mrs. Bernard Madoff

I acknowledge the legacy of shame I have created for my family.

—Bernard Madoff

In this fantasy analysis, the therapist makes use of the language of dialectics to show the two sides of Mrs. Madoff—how she knew and at the same time did not know what her husband was doing.

Therapist (Th): Mrs. Madoff, I can hear the grief and shock you experienced upon hearing about your husband's crimes and his arrest.

Mrs. Madoff
(Mrs. M): Shock isn't the word. I had no idea he was involved in these scandals.

Th: You are not the only one who is a victim of your husband's fraud. Others claim that this is their worst nightmare. One woman who trusted your husband felt like her life was shattered when she discovered that all of her mother's investments were lost, as well as her entire inheritance.

Mrs. M: Really? I had no clue. Bernie is basically a really good person. He gave to charities, cared about people, and was a good husband and family man.

Th: But the victims choked and sobbed when they heard about the magnitude of their losses. Some people even said that his jail would become his coffin. The losses in the Ponzi scheme were over 50 billion dollars!

Mrs. M: Maybe so, but I don't think he deserves 150 years in jail.

Th: He is a criminal.

Mrs. M: But he is not the ordinary type of criminal. He did not enjoy watching people suffer like Charles Manson. He just got carried away.

Th: Here I do have to agree with you. He was not the typical sadistic criminal who enjoyed watching people writhe in pain. He got lost in his greed and, once he saw that he could get away with his Ponzi scheme, he became insatiable. There was no stopping him.

Mrs. M: I am glad you understand that.

Th: There is a difference, but, unfortunately, that does not hold up in court.

Mrs. M: At least he apologized and realized the pain and suffering he caused.

Th: He also caused you pain and suffering. I guess it was hard for you to face what was going on. Certainly after being married 50 years you must have had some sense that something wasn't right.

Mrs. M: I did have a feeling but didn't pay much attention. Our lives were so good. We lived on a beautiful estate, had many homes, and I was enjoying a wonderful lifestyle with him and our family. I could shop anytime I felt like it, and I love to shop.

Th: I guess you became insatiable as well with your shopping, and it was hard to face the undeniable fear that there was some serious fraud going on.

Mrs. M: I am not the only one who was fooled. Bernie has an amazing gift of getting everyone to trust him. He would even tell people when not to invest, which made people trust him even more (the false self).

Th: But your sons knew about this and even reported him.

Mrs. M: Well, I guess I got lost and couldn't face what was going on. I was enjoying the luxury in our lives, and when I shop I think of nothing else. I guess I am a shopaholic.

Th: And your husband became a fraudaholic. This is where you both went astray. You both got lost in your grandiose schemes, and your voracious selves made you lose your realities (ego dysfunctionality within the dance of the couple).

Mrs. M: Now I have lost everything: all our homes, including our $7 million penthouse in New York, and all our personal property.

Th: How ironic! With all the shopping, you thought you would gain something, but instead it turned out to be a huge loss. This sense of entitlement you and your husband share led to complete devastation and irrevocable losses. We need to stop now but, in the meantime, I will refer you to a bereavement group to deal with these feelings of loss and mourning and also continue your treatment to help you mourn the pain.

The purpose of this fantasy analysis was not to show empathy for Mrs. Madoff's denial, since she was an active participant in her husband's wrongdoings, but to provide some understanding of how they joined together in a *folie à deux* motivated by their shared uncontrollable, insatiable needs, greed, and grandiose entitlement fantasies.

Many borderlines enrage or humiliate their partners, exhibit poor hygiene, dress sloppily or inappropriately, and show very little concern for their appearance. Many even become reverse snobs: "Why should I dress up for those assholes?" To illustrate the contrast, Mahari introduces us to the "quiet borderline," a far cry from the malignant one who is downright loud and "in your face." Clinically, I have come to know the "quiet borderline," who exhibits very similar characteristics to the passive–aggressive personality. On the surface they are "the good little boys" who can do no wrong, but because of their forgetfulness, "do-it-mañana" attitude, or lack of initiative, they evoke rage in their partners. "You are the bad mommy always angry with me, and I'm just the good little husband (or wife) who didn't do anything wrong." One woman reported that her husband would play stimulating games with their sons, but when it came to any discipline he did not think it was his responsibility.

Because overlapping traits and symptoms have made it difficult to distinguish the malignant borderline from the malignant narcissist (and even from the sociopath and antisocial narcissist), I have had to draw from my work on terrorism to come up with a description and differential diagnosis. As a psychohistorian studying terrorism, counterterrorism, and suicide bombers in conjunction with my good friend and colleague Nancy Kobrin (the author of *The Banality of Suicide Terrorism*, 2010), I have found a parallel between domestic abuse and global terrorism (Kobrin & Lachkar, 2005). Kobrin came to the rescue as she plowed through numerous case studies comparing domestic violence to terrorism. Together we speculated and asked the obvious questions: What does global terrorism have to do with domestic violence? How would one treat a terrorist?

In my earlier works (Lachkar, 2002, 2006, 2008c), I describe terrorists as having a predominantly collective borderline disorder—which would explain how entire nations, such as those under Islamic regimes, are drawn to identify with destructive, tyrannical leaders. These leaders appear to be acting out father figure/savior fantasies for an entire group of lost, abandoned "orphan babies" suffering from severe feelings of loss, fear of imminent danger (real or imagined), deprivation, and trauma resulting from early child-rearing practices. Just as individuals identify with certain abusive partners in a domestic relationship, so do groups and nations identify with paranoid, destructive tyrannical leaders. In short, without sounding too grandiose, I reasoned that if this is the case for global terrorists, why would it not apply to domestic ones?

The malignant borderline exhibits extreme paranoid and antisocial features. This type of borderline is the most malicious and abusive, and the source of domestic violence, abuse, and terrorism (moving from the domestic to the global). They are basically evil, with no sense of conscience or morality. Under the guise of "the cause," they will act out their most heinous crimes. The need to retaliate and exact revenge becomes all-encompassing. These are the most toxic type of borderlines; they are pathological liars, manipulators, suffer from paranoia, exhibit a high level of distrust, and maliciously distort the good intentions of others. Often they are cult-like or tyrannical leaders such as Slobodan Milosevic, Saddam Hussein, or Osama bin Laden (Lachkar, 2000).

Malignant borderlines often engage in violence and terrorism and exhibit a sadistic superego—unleashed aggression that has run amok. It is as though they have no filter that allows them to understand the consequences of their actions; they are more preoccupied with repeating the trauma of abuse. Ethnic cleansing is an example of the type of guilt they display—for example, the Germans tried to cleanse themselves by getting rid of the "dirty Jews," and the Serbs by getting rid of the intrusive "dirty" Kosovos. "Save Serbia!" "Destroy the dirty Jews, then we (the Germans) can regain our purity and freedom from contamination."

Individuals who identify with abusive and destructive leaders (Adolf Hitler, Saddam Hussein, Slobodan Milosevic) play out certain group fantasies to express the group's conscious or unconscious yearnings and strivings. In regressive groups, the pull of playing out these collective group fantasies is overpowering. Group members will subject themselves to anything (including death, suicide, deprivation, and self-sacrifice) to remain forever loyal and faithful to an idealized charismatic leader. Historically, we have witnessed time and again how some paranoid or delusional leader can mesmerize an entire nation, putting people in a "trance" that reinforces the group's already existing mythological collective group fantasies. "I am your savior, the father you never had. I will save you from nothingness and fear, and bring purpose and meaning into your lives. But first we must bond together and destroy the infidels, the bad 'She'—America, our infinite enemy." (Lachkar, 2004b, p. 127).

Umar Adulmutallab, the Nigerian Christmas Day bomber (2009) who tried to blow up the Detroit-bound U.S. airplane, is described as a deprived, sexually frustrated man, a loner who nurtured fantasies about holy war. In his twisted mind he finds justification for his destructive, aggressive impulses through jihad fantasies. He believes his actions will return the Muslim world once again to the status of a great empire. "Killing is permitted in jihad." One could speculate whether he is a peace-loving Muslim out to give his life for a cause, or if he is acting out his anger and internal terror through the organized brotherhood. Is he intentionally cruel and sadistic, a global abuser partner? Tentatively, I opt for the latter, that the cruelty is disguised/assuaged under the banner of jihad, but that in reality he is a loner finding an outlet for revenge.

Do terrorists have a superego? A conscience? Are they able to express remorse? The answer is yes, but they listen to a different voice. In the spirit of Islam and the brotherhood, they find justification for massacre, torture, degradation, and punishment. But as bad as they are, they must answer to some higher power (e.g., Allah, "Allah Akbar!" meaning "God is great!"). Another example of assuaging guilt is by identifying with an idealized figure like Slobodan Milosevic. According to deMause (2007), the malignant borderline maintains a fusion with the Killer Mother, joined by the Bad Self little boy. In order to protect her, he must kill off his enemies. In this primitive state the country becomes the mother (e.g., The Motherland, Germany *uber alles*), and he will kill off "her" enemies or die for her. In the case of the Muslims, the killer boy resurrects the abandoned father, Mohammed/Allah, and will do anything to fight against everyone and anyone who gives even the slightest suggestion of an insult (e.g., the Danish cartoons that caused such an uproar).

The Malignant Borderline as a Domestic Abuser

The difference between a malignant borderline as a domestic perpetrator and as a terrorist is that the former acts out aggressive impulses without thought, whereas the terrorist is able to restrict his urges and impulses to an organized, systematic structure within the framework of the brotherhood. I take the liberty of making a further distinction between the domestic malignant borderline and the terrorist by noting that their actions depend on the level of superego functioning. This does not mean that behind closed doors men can act out their most heinous abuse against women (stoning, cutting off their hands, divorcing on a whim). Some say terrorists have no conscience. They find justification for actions, hiding behind the banner of a cause to provide superego relief. "We are not terrorists! We are freedom fighters and keepers of peace!" The only time they express remorse is when they have failed or disappointed. At the domestic level, a good example of this is the accused killer, Scott Roeder, on trial for first-degree murder in the 2009 shooting death of Dr. George Tiller at an abortion clinic (fighting for a "cause to save the lives of unborn fetuses").

Malignant borderlines are inextricably linked to violence and abuse, both physical and emotional. In contrast to the pathological borderline, malignant borderlines are the ones who torment their partners. In couples therapy, their partners often live in terror. Malignant borderlines withhold money, humiliate and shame their partners publicly, and in some cases burn, beat, mutilate, and intentionally subject their partners to severe torture and violence. They may resort to such acts as raping and killing.

Therapists and friends are often baffled as to why people stick around and subject themselves to the abuse. This is where the language of dialectics becomes effective. As bad as these perpetrators may be as the cruel abuser, they can also be loving and kind. This creates confusion and ambivalence (Lachkar, 2008a, 2008b). Many of these abusers play a role that moves back and forth between sadist and lover. "Come here, honey. You know I didn't mean to throw you against the wall. You know I love you!" This becomes a dance between the victim and the abuser, a dance between the dialectic of love and cruelty.

Although domestic abusers will act out impulsively, they later will show remorse and beg for forgiveness, promising that this will never happen again. This is why people stay—because their apologies are convincing. However, lack of impulse control prevents the malignant borderline from following through on promises. In many of my earlier works, I have referred to this as the "dance," how the borderline's seductive promises lure their partners back into the relationship. "I love you, honey. I promise this will never happen again." A good example is the high profile case of Chris Brown and his abusive relationship with Rihanna, how he brutally beat her, showed remorse, and how she returned to him before she summoned the courage to leave for good. If Chris Brown were in therapy, how would we communicate? First, we would need to understand the level of his superego function and ability for impulse control. "Even though you express remorse, at the time you were not able to listen to the voice inside that tells you it is okay to want to beat up your partner but not okay to do it."

The Role of the V-Spot

Malignant borderlines prey on their victims by attacking their most sensitive area of emotional vulnerability—the V-spot. The V-spot parallels the G-spot. (The G-spot equals pleasure, the V-spot equals pain.) It is the raw area of the psyche that is aroused when one triggers a traumatic experience related to painful memory traces of early childhood, or when someone we love hits our hypersensitive core. I refer to this as the archaic area of vulnerability (Lachkar, 2008b), which is easily subject to attack, evoking a disproportionately explosive reaction. The V-spot can blow with seemingly the slightest event! One wrong word, one false move, and it's off! The V-spot is the epicenter of our most fragile area, known in psychoanalytic literature as the "archaic injury." It is a product of early trauma that one unwittingly holds onto and maintains throughout adult life. I devised the term *V-spot* because it is more user-friendly than "archaic injury" and makes it easier to pinpoint the vertex or exact area of vulnerability.

Does each disorder have its own archaic injury? I believe the answer is yes. For example, the narcissist may blow when not properly mirrored, the borderline when feeling abandoned or betrayed, the obsessive–compulsive when emotions get out of control, and the passive–aggressive when met with excessive demands (Lachkar, 2008a).

Getting in contact with the area of vulnerability is the only way to help victims break away from emotional abuse and activate the healing process. In emotionally abusive relationships, the V-spot is stimulated and aroused again and again. Understanding their V-spot helps patients find their "powerhouse." It is to the psyche what yoga, Pilates, spinning, kick boxing, and other power workouts are to our muscles. Finding and making use of the V-spot involves an intense emotional workout that strengthens and emotionally renews the individual. It is the beginning of the healing process. One patient put it this way after she found out how to make contact with her vulnerable spot:

> I never could understand why I would stay with a man who abuses me and threatens to kill me if I don't comply with his wishes. When I don't comply, he takes revenge against our kids, keeping me in a state of complete helplessness. I was beginning to feel that I was bad and deserving of the abuse, that everything was my fault, that I deserved my husband's violent temper and mistreatment. Now all I do is turn to my V-spot, and as soon as I get in contact with it my thought processes clear up. I talk to my V-spot now all the time, and realize that my thoughts are my defenses and not my real feelings. Even if I am the worst person in the world, I am not deserving of this kind of terrorism.

What about the perpetrator of the terror? Does he have a V-spot? Yes, but of a different nature. At least the abused wife is in contact with her V-spot, whereas her spouse is highly disassociated from it and does not have the emotional resources or ego strength to get in contact with it. He is too afraid. The malignant borderline cannot tolerate feeling vulnerable or dependent, so defends against this by becoming aggressive or a bully, trying to exact revenge on the world. They delude themselves into thinking that, if they can control, dominate, and put the fear of God into their victims, they will be big and powerful. The superego operates at the most primitive level and has not advanced to the level of maturity; instead it is sadistic, overly harsh, and severe. "I cannot tolerate my own weakness, so when I see others around me as victims or as needy and dependent, I will destroy them." The following is an example of a domestic malignant borderline.

Case of Bonnie and Joe

In the case that follows, the focus is on Bonnie. The therapist moves away from "how to communicate" and concentrates on safety and security for Bonnie and her child, while helping her regain her power and self-esteem, and confronting the delusion that she is helpless and powerless.

Bonnie has been trying to separate from Joe, but fears if she does he will threaten her, beat her, and do everything he can to get his revenge—even take away their four-year-old son. Joe has done everything he can to defeat Bonnie. He has been frivolously spending the money she earns from her job on Harleys, going out and entertaining other women lavishly, buying high-tech equipment, including what she refers to as the "fuck phone" to contact these other women. When Bonnie confronts Joe, he looks at her as if she is some alien from outer space.

> *Bonnie (B):* He did it again.
> *Therapist (Th):* Silent.
> *B:* I found the fuck phone and all the numbers he's been calling.
> *Th:* So, he has been lying to you again?
> *B:* Yes!
> *Th:* You seem surprised!
> *B:* Actually, I'm not. I am beginning to see he is a pathological liar.
> *Th:* This is a shift from thinking that you are deserving of this kind of violence and mistreatment.
> *B:* I am making progress, but I am still concerned. When I confront him, he either storms out of the house or puts the fear of God into me.
> *Th:* He got caught!
> *B:* He can't face what he has done to me. He spends all my hard-earned money. I get up at 5 in the morning, take our son to school, work as an administrator all day, pick up our son, cook, shop, do endless paperwork. I am exhausted, and then I have to deal with him.

Th: Of all the work you have to do, nothing is more exhausting than to live in constant fear and terror.

B: But even worse is how he invalidates my perception and makes me feel as though I am crazy. So, you are the communications expert! What do I say to him?

Th: Bonnie, this goes beyond communication. The first priority is your safety. He has shut doors in your face, locked you out of the house, slammed you against the wall, hit you in front of your son.

B: Are you suggesting I call the police?

Th: I would say yes, but first you need to know the ramifications. Before you do anything, we need to ensure your safety.

B: If I call the police, that could make things worse. He is a civil employee. If he gets a criminal record, he won't be able to work again (a real therapeutic dilemma for many therapists).

Th: Then you will need to go to a safe place like Sojourn, a place for women who are being abused. They will help you as they do many other women in your situation. You are not alone.

B: I know you are right, but I just can't bring myself to do this.

Th: Why?

B: I am afraid to be alone, let alone deal with the stigma and shame of being a single woman.

Th: So your choice is to stay with someone who beats you, threatens you, spends your money on Harleys and then runs around calling on his fuck phone.

B: I'm scared.

Th: Good that you are scared. It is appropriate for you to be scared. That is different from being helpless and powerless and feeling that there is nothing you can do. You must regain your power.

B: So trying to talk to him you don't think will help.

Th: Bonnie, right now I am trying to "talk" to you!

Case of Maureen and Tony

The case of Maureen and Tony illustrates the importance of bonding with the perpetrator in order to establish a working therapeutic alliance. Maureen requested that Tony set up an appointment for conjoint treatment. This case is an illustration of how the therapist becomes a "Winnicottian mother," helping the couples distinguish the act of "being" from the act of "doing." Using the "language of dialectics," the therapist attempts to help the couple sort out the differences within the drama of their enactments.

> *Tony:* (Call to therapist prior to session.) I suppose you think I am a real monster.
>
> *Therapist (Th):* Actually, it is the opposite. Maureen was telling me how successful and how very accomplished you are. Not easy to become CEO of a major music company, especially given the trauma and losses in your life.
>
> *Tony:* So, she didn't tell you about the things I've done?
>
> *Th:* Yes, but when you are here I have a chance to hear your story.
>
> *Th:* (In session.) Who would like to start?
>
> *Tony:* Well, things are not going so well. Maureen is refusing to cook and could care less what we eat. She'd be happy eating shit!
>
> *Maureen:* Oh, is that why you dumped our dog's poop in the trash can next to my bed?
>
> *Tony:* I had no choice. You don't listen to reason or any logic.
>
> *Maureen:* Logic! You think you have logic? How about the time I came home and you locked the dog in the closet? That was really cruel.
>
> *Th:* I think you are letting me know that all you give each other in the relationship is poop, and I am here to help clean you both up. Maureen, you feel that all you get is poop from Tony, and, Tony, your wife keeps you stuck and locked in like the dog. These are legitimate feelings, but the actions are not acceptable. Besides, attack, revenge, cruelty is only going to create more poop.
>
> *Tony:* So, what shall we do?
>
> *Th:* Eating shit is not the same as feeling like shit, so before we decide what to do, we need to understand how you are each replaying unconscious trauma from the past that keeps you both stuck in a toilet bowl. My job is to help you get out of it.

In this case, the movements become a dialectic dance between the act of being and the act of doing. The therapist struggles to find a way to let the couples know that is okay to feel like shit, but it is not okay to actually produce it. The attempt to give advice is put aside to first allow each partner to ponder how they unconsciously play out some unresolved primitive issue in the other. Although this does not directly deal with torture or criminality, Tony's cruelty contains many of the elements of the malignant borderline as he crosses the perimeter of the silent borderline (the borderline who in his silence or "good little boy" mode sets his partner up to enact his repressed rage).

Women Who Choose to Stay With Malignant Borderlines

Who are the people who get hooked up with malignant borderlines, and what kind of reactions do they provoke in others? In my earlier contribution, *The Many Faces of Abuse* (1998a, 2004a), I discussed a certain type of high-functioning women whose guilt is shaded by shame, which keeps her locked in an abusive relationship. (Although the focus is primarily on men being the perpetrators, certainly this can also apply to women as well.) According to recent surveys, it is estimated that one-fifth of U.S. women experience domestic violence, and it is more often men who are the perpetrators; it is also more often the women who fall prey to this form of psychological domination. Kernberg (1991, 1992, 1995) claims that men who are more often the perpetrators, tend to be more sadistic, have a proclivity toward violence, and women are more masochistic. He claims that it is the men's insecurity, seeing women as inferior, which has its origins in the envy of pregential mother. Often people are shocked to find out that she remains in an emotionally or physically abusive relationship. "What! You are a lawyer and you subject yourself to this kind of abuse?" "A doctor! Shouldn't you know better!" Many of these abused women are not hampered by a lack of intelligence, or what they claim is "their stupidity." Rather, there is a sense of shame that they are not powerful or strong enough to confront their abuser because they feel enslaved by the terror and because they often feel deserving of the abuse (Lachkar, 1998a). Although these women are admired because of their success, they also evoke an inordinate amount of envy in their partner, and thus they must be destroyed. "Just because she is a hot-shot lawyer, what gives her the right to tell me what to do!"

Although any woman can get hooked into an abusive relationship, the borderline attracts certain kinds of partners. Typically, the type of woman who stays with a malignant borderline is someone who displays a borderline pathology, is dependent, or assumes a caretaker role. Another type of woman who joins up with this disorder's pathogenesis is someone who displaces unwanted aggressive parts of herself onto her partner to act out her repressed and unleashed anger and rage. Often these women do not have a sense of self but will collude with their abuser to either maintain a sense of existence or because of abandonment issues. "I know my husband committed many crimes, but he did them for a good cause." Another common reason is fear. Some are just too terrified to leave. The daunting endless threats will cause the woman to stay for fear of her life. She is caught in a Catch-22. She is doomed if she stays, and she is doomed if she leaves. That is why it is useful to suggest that before the woman makes any criminal charges she should first be assured that she will be in a safe place, out of harm's way.

Treating the Severest Forms of Malignant Borderline Syndrome

Our consultation settings are, generally speaking, not designed to treat extremely severe cases of malignant borderline syndrome (terrorists, murderers). Yet officials in our law enforcement and judicial systems—ranging from local police and courts to homeland security—do have the need for an in-depth understanding of the dynamics that underlie the malignant borderline. This is useful not only in thwarting crime but also in apprehending criminals and dealing with them most effectively.

In order to understand the destructive nature of criminality, it is useful to turn to Melanie Klein's (1927) concept of on criminality in children. One of her greatest contributions to play therapy was to allow the freedom and space to develop fantasy life in children. She recognized that children have all kinds of sadistic fantasies about mutilating, destroying, killing. But the children gradually learn to differentiate enactment from fantasy. In short, it is okay to "think it" (cut mother's breast or mutilate daddy's penis), but it is not okay to "do it" (fantasy versus reality). Many murderers, pedophiles, perverts grow up without learning this distinction. Klein emphasizes how criminals ward off anxiety by blocking out guilt emanating from the super-ego. As an example, I compare the primitive mind to the abstract mind of Abraham, who realized early on that he did not actually have to sacrifice Isaac but could substitute the act with a ram—a concept missing in the mind of a criminal. These concepts might be important for trial lawyers, judges, probation officers, and others, including mental health professionals treating the families of criminals, criminals in jail or out on probation. People such as Charles Manson and Susan Atkins do not have to actually have to cut, slice, or mutilate their victims as if they are slicing a turkey; they can fantasize about it but not actually do it. Criminals whose minds have not progressed beyond primitive reasoning to mature reasoning cannot distinguish the act of "being or feeling" from the act of "doing." "I feel; therefore I do it."

Summary

Communicating effectively with a domestic abuser or terrorist requires that we address the shame behind their deeds. We need to let them know that as children they were not responsible for the abuse or traumas bestowed upon them. Yet it must be stated that destructive behaviors reinforce the shame and recreate the very thing that the malignant borderline tries to avoid: it reinforces their false sense of power. We would consistently address the shame and envy, assuring them that one should not have to feel shame in conjunction with the betraying mother or the abandoning father or any childhood abuse, that they are not responsible for the crimes of their parents. Although many of us are not treating terrorists, we may be consulting with people working in government agencies, law enforcement, homeland security, the justice system, prisons. As the world changes around us, we must be equipped to deal with the new wave of violence and aggression—typically perpetrated by the malignant borderline—that we face both domestically and globally.

5

The Depressive Borderline

In my earlier work, *How to Talk to a Narcissist* (2008b), I describe how depressive narcissistic disturbances occur when the narcissist is depleted of his/her narcissistic supplies—e.g., loss of power, fame, youth, money—and has exhausted his/her narcissistic suppliers (self-objects that support and mirror them). This is in sharp contrast to the depressive borderline, who does not feel depleted because he or she never had or wanted power, fame, or money in the first place. Where narcissists are concerned about proving a special sense of existence, evidenced by their successes and possessions, borderlines are busy trying to prove they exist in and of themselves. "When I cut my wrists, it hurts; but at least I know I am alive." Proving their existence becomes the most compelling force in the borderline's narrow world (Lachkar, 2008b).

Thus, we invite another disorder to the "Land of Borderville"—the depressive borderline, or should we say, a borderline with symptoms of depression. Depression in borderline pathology is inextricably linked to clinical conditions where loss of an early object plays an important role. We have noted that many borderlines have had losses in early life and stay unconsciously and internally identified with the lost object. They are immobilized and stuck in their world of interjections and projections; characterized by low self-esteem and chronic negativity, they are doomed to failure and are overly judgmental of themselves and others. They are pessimistic, lack trust, are socially isolated, joyless, and fill their days with gloom, despair, and bouts of morbidity. They project these aspects and create pain and negativity in the people around them, who get frustrated with their shame/blame defenses, anger, and aggression.

In treatment, they are most taxing on the therapist's empathy because whatever help or advice they receive is readily repudiated. "I already know that. I already tried that. Stop bugging me! Don't you know that whatever I do will lead to rejection?" People with borderline personality disorder (BPD) exhibit highly unstable relations that are changeable (all good one moment and all bad the next). The most pervasive feature of depressed borderlines is the inclination to attack themselves (self-hatred turned inward). Not having a well-integrated sense of self leaves them feeling worthless and inadequate. Many have depleted their objects or exhausted them with their complaints, self-pity, hypochondrias, and victimization. They constantly complain about people who they feel do not understand them or care about them, mistreat them, or just plainly reject them. Because they are so hard on themselves, they also are hard on others and become overly self-righteous. These individuals will often unknowingly go on and on negatively about their pains, woes, or problems (almost like a reverse narcissist), and then wonder why people get annoyed, angry, or frustrated with them. Like other borderlines discussed in this book, they lack the observing ego to monitor their own process. On a more precautionary note, it is important for clinicians to be willing to explore this dark side. "No! It is not your needs that turn people off. Your needs are healthy. It is your constant barrage of complaints that has the effect of making others leery of you. Then you wonder why you are lonely."

Pressures the Depressive Borderline Places on Others

Because of the depressive borderline's pervasive sense of joylessness and negativity, they tend not only to make themselves miserable, helpless, and frustrated, but they sabotage any joy or potential happiness in their partners and those who interact with them. They wear out their objects because they are just as hard on others as they are critical of themselves. One woman attacked her husband for always getting crumbs on the floor. He retorted, "Judy, just because you feel crummy, you accuse me of being the one dropping the crumbs!"

> *Mr. W. asks a woman on a date. At the restaurant he stares at the menu and can't decide what to order. The server comes to take their order and again he stares at the menu. "I'm really not hungry. I'll just have a glass of water. The date never returns his calls and Mr. W. wonders why.*

Ms. G. goes to an audition. The director asks her to read her part with a Spanish accent. When she didn't get the part, Ms. G. went home, got into bed, and stayed there for two days; she couldn't sleep or eat, and felt completely paralyzed. When asked why she took not getting the part so much to heart, especially when speaking with a Spanish accent was not part of her repertoire, she responded, "I just hate myself. I know I should have studied Spanish. Now I am a complete screw-up."

What follows are examples of the depressive borderline's harsh, critical, judgmental, unleashed superego:

Mrs. P is a recovering alcoholic who has been sober for three years. When she goes to a party and sees her friends drinking, she thinks nothing of going over to them and saying, "Don't you know better than to drink in front of my face? You know I can't drink and am trying hard to maintain my sobriety!" Mrs. P. does not have the slightest idea why her friends get irritated and find her intrusive and controlling. She just marks them off as being rude and inconsiderate.

Mrs. S. invites her friend for dinner at a restaurant to celebrate her friend's birthday. When the bill comes, she asks her friend to split it. The friend politely pays her share but then never has anything more to do with Mrs. S. Mrs. S. does not have the slightest hint as to why her friend was annoyed, and wonders why she always ends up feeling lonely and rejected.

Diagnostic Criteria (DSM-IV, Appendix B)

Depressive Borderline

The *Diagnostic and Statistical Manual of Mental Disorders*, 4th Edition, Text Revision (DSM-IV-TR), a widely used manual for diagnosing mental disorders, defines *depressive personality* disorder as:

A. A pervasive pattern of depressive cognitions and behaviors beginning by early adulthood and present in a variety of contexts, as indicated by five (or more) of the following:
   1. Moods are dominated by dejection, gloominess, cheerlessness, joylessness, unhappiness.
   2. Self-concept centers around beliefs of inadequacy, worthlessness, and low self-esteem.

3. Overly critical, blaming, and derogatory toward self.
4. Constant brooding, worry over future and potential disaster.
5. Critical and negative and negativistic and judgmental towards others.
6. Pessimistic.
7. Critical superego, guilt and cannot take advice from others.

B. Condition does not occur exclusively during major depressive episodes and is not better accounted for by dysthymic disorder.

Other Symptoms and Signs of the Depressive Borderline
- Putting pressure on others
- Destroying the joy
- Exhibiting irritable moods
- Lacking passion and enthusiasm
- Showing low or no sex drive
- Bonding with pain
- Preoccupation with feeling sorry for themselves

Borderline depression occurs when the borderline has depleted and exhausted all his or her objects with negativity and complaints. Because of the lack of impulse control and splitting mechanism, the borderline cannot maintain the continuity and ego strength an intimate relationship requires. When the false self runs out of fuel, and the attacking, victimized, shameful self emerges as the true self, the person often falls into a state of borderline depression—a persecutory superego ridden with shame and unresolved residue of guilt.

This is a mental disorder characterized by an all-pervasive low mood accompanied by low self-esteem or loss of interest or pleasure. Similar to other BPD types, they sabotage and destroy the joy and pleasure of those around them. The difference is that other borderlines sabotage because they have difficulty following through with commitments, whereas the depressive borderline cannot follow through with commitments because of guilt emanating from a critical superego, which prevents him/her from experiencing the "good life."

"I am not good enough! I don't deserve to have fun. I should have invested in the company stock. Why didn't I do that? Why am I such a screwup?" It becomes a mantra of self-blame. "Oh, why? Oh, why?" Depressives are also the pessimists; every piece of mail, every phone call, every event is tantamount to doom and failure.

Sue wants to get married. Mike wants to as well, but worries he won't have enough money to support a wife and potentially a family. Sue reassures Mike that his parents are going to leave him a big inheritance and that he is making enough money to pursue a medical practice. "Oh, but what if there is a depression?" What if I get sick? What if my parents decide to leave all their money to my brother?" Sue was beginning to suspect that Mike suffers from depression. She noted that his concerns were not only about possible future losses related to big issues; he would show the same concern for minor things. "I don't know if this new TV is a good choice. I should have checked into it more. I am so stupid! Why did I buy this? I am going to try and return it." Sue says that everything Mike buys, he questions, deliberates about, and then self-blames, so that even shopping at the market becomes a joyless and burdensome task.

Overlap

Different Kinds of Depression

Normal depression is a response to something tragic that everyone in life has to deal with at some time—loss of a parent or spouse, a breakup, or loss of an opportunity. People within the normal range of mental health will, of course, feel sadness and grieve over their losses; but they will not feel persecuted and will somehow manage to go on with their lives. They momentarily rely on others to help them get through the crisis (support groups, friends, and family members). Major depression is a disabling condition that adversely affects a person's family, work, or school life, as well as sleeping and eating habits, and general health. In the United States, approximately 3.4 percent of people with major depression commit suicide, and up to 60 percent of people who commit suicide have depression or another mood disorder.

It is important to know the differences between the types of depression common to most human beings, as distinguished from those caused by a chemical imbalance or clinical or major depression.

General Depression

The term *depression* is often used to describe a mood disorder in general terms. A person who is depressed is continually down on himself, feels sad and blue, and projects into those around him that the world is a bad and dismal place. *General depression* is also a term that interfaces with other personality disorders in that it is not as disabling or crippling as major depression, which affects a person's ability to function (sex drive, social life, work, and school). Many people who are depressed can also function at a very high level. "I am depressed, but I can still get up in the morning and go to work!"

In order for us to have a better perspective, let us now take a look at the paranoid–schizoid position as a state that precedes the depressive position.

Paranoid–Schizoid Position

The paranoid–schizoid position is a fragmented position in which thoughts and feelings are split off and projected because the psyche cannot tolerate feelings of pain, emptiness, loneliness, rejection, humiliation, or ambiguity. It is dominated primarily by part-object functioning and shame/blame defenses. "When I hit that runway, I only see myself as an ugly little girl; I cannot see myself today as a top model." Klein viewed this position as the earliest phase of development, part-object functioning, and the beginning of the primitive superego (undeveloped) (Klein, 1984). If the child views mother as a "good breast," the child will maintain good, warm, and hopeful feelings about his/her environment. If, on the other hand, the infant experiences mother as a "bad breast," the child is more likely to experience the environment as bad, attacking, and persecutory. Klein, more than any of her followers, understood the primary importance of the need for mother and the breast.

Case Example: Brian and Joanne

Brian is a surgeon who, after taking numerous sleeping medications the night before, wakes up every morning bleary eyed and exhausted from tossing and turning all night. When he gets up, he tells his wife about the horrific night he has experienced and how he is doomed and does not know how he is going to get through the day with his surgeries. Brian, repeatedly, like a mantra, complains to his wife about how depressed he is and how he does not know how long he will last at the hospital and that she needs to be careful about spending any money.

>   *Joanne (J):* Well, here we are again. Brian woke up this morning depressed and didn't sleep. It is difficult because he keeps me up all night, and I have to get up early with the kids.

Therapist (Th): Yes, here you are again. It does sound like an ongoing issue.

Brian (B): A lot of this is my fault. I am just a loser. Everything I do turns to crap.

Th: Oh!

B: I tried to get a promotion at the hospital, and now they tell me I will have to wait for my evaluation. I know it will be terrible.

J: This is what he does. He always is pessimistic and sees the future as doom and despair.

Th: Brian, Joanne has a point. Are you conscious of your attitude about life?

B: Not really. It is true, though. I have no future. I just know what my superiors will say. They will find me incompetent. I come in every day red-eyed and exhausted.

Th: It really is remarkable, because from what I hear when you hit the examination table you are a master. Your surgeries have been impeccable.

J: They really are. In fact, other doctors come to Brian for consultation, especially for complex bypass surgeries.

B: That's true, but it still doesn't matter. I just know they will not give me a promotion.

Th: Why?

B: Because that's how I feel, that's why. So don't push it!

Th: I guess I do need to push it. If you didn't want me to push it, then you wouldn't be here.

J: Yeah! I wish I had said that!

Th: You wish you had said that because Brian feels he is doomed, and anyone who confronts that is doomed as well.

B: Okay, so tell me what you were going to say.

Th: Brian, you are confusing how you feel with the way things are (distorted reality).

B: Now you tell me I am confused. I thought I was bad enough.

Th: Brian, you are not bad, and I did not say you are confused. I said you are confusing your inner feelings with reality. How you feel and how things really are don't match up.

J: That's what he does all the time—attacks me.

Th: Joanne, I think he is just as harsh with you as he is with himself.

B: This is how it's been my whole life. Don't think I can change things now.

Th: Maybe we can't change you, but what we can do is help you see yourself more realistically so that you do not view the world as so bleak.

B: Look, I lost my father when I was two years old. He died in an automobile accident. No wonder I am depressed. How do you expect me to feel?

Th: Brian, this is not depression. Your feelings are normal. You are dealing with loss, loss of the most important person in your life—your father. So rather than deal with the mourning and loss, you have turned against yourself, making yourself into a bad little boy. This is not depression! This is intense sadness, and it *feels* bad!

B: Interesting you say that because I notice that when I am praised or other doctors come to me for consultation, I think they're nuts. Don't they see I am just a bad little boy that does not deserve their recognition?

J: Brian, I wish you could express yourself like this more often. I believe what I am hearing is that because you feel bad you become the badness that you feel. Is that right?

Th: Exactly! This is not unusual with early losses. Little children do not understand that they were not the cause of the death or the accident, and often spend the rest of their lives with unresolved guilt. As a surgeon, you must not "bypass" this.

B: Now who's the surgeon?

Th: Me! I am the surgeon doing psychological surgery, cutting away parts that do not belong inside of you.

J: Thank you. This has been so helpful. So I should not personalize his negativity.

Th: Not if you want to have a good night's sleep and a healthy heart. See you both next week.

J and B: Bye now.

Discussion

This case demonstrates how the therapist navigates the language of dialectics in communicating with Brian, whose inner self is in complete conflict with his outer self. Because he feels like a bad boy, Brian thinks he *is* a bad boy (confusing inner self with outer self). Brian's primitive defenses are clearly in the paranoid–schizoid position, the way he perceives himself as a part-loss object and then projects onto others so that they will see him as a bad child. Note how the therapist avoided getting into a battle, instead transforming the idea of "change" into the concept of helping him see things more clearly. As one of my analytic supervisors so wisely said, "A soldier fights; a psychoanalyst interprets." The effort on the part of the therapist is to help Brian see himself as the capable and high-functioning man that he is—a whole object, with the ability to hold onto the good and whole aspects of the self.

The Depressive Position

The depressive position is not to be confused with major or clinical depression. Therapists cannot ignore the work of Melanie Klein, and her valuable approach to understanding the various kinds of depressive disorders described in this chapter. Many patients diagnosed with general or major depression fit more snugly into the category of Klein's (1957) *depressive position*. This is a term devised by Klein to describe a state of mourning and sadness in which integration and reparation take place. The benefits of the depressive position as outlined by Klein transform the "label" of depression into a concept more palatable—sadness, loss, and mourning. Sadness is not pathological and is considered by Klein as a healthy and higher level of development (Klein, 1948). In this stage, not everything is seen in terms of black and white. Primarily it is a whole object position whereby one sees self, and others, as not all good or bad but as a more integrated self. There is more tolerance, guilt, remorse, self-doubt, frustration, pain, and confusion in this position. One is more responsible for one's actions. There is the realization not of what things should be but the way they are. As verbal expression increases, one may still feel sadness, but one may also feel a newly regained sense of aliveness.

The movements back and forth between inner and outer hatred toward the self can lead to severe depression. It is imperative for the therapist to help the depressive borderline recognize that this portion of his low moods is not to be confused with healthy states of mourning and loss. The second area of frustration is the need to meet the standard absolute perfection. Anything less than perfect is thought to be devalued; therefore, the person tends to give up and not pursue the challenges of real life. "Why should I try? Everything I do leads to failure." The most pressing problem with the depressive borderline is the frustration evoked not only in therapists but in those who live and interact with these borderlines.

The depressive position as postulated by Klein is a high point in one's development. It is the stage in which one moves away from the paranoid–schizoid position of shame/blame and mania to a state of sadness and mourning. It is a time of remorse, during which one comes to terms with wrongdoings and the wish to make reparation. When patients complain to the therapist that they are getting worse instead of better because their moods have declined and they are feeling interminably sad and depressed, this is a time for celebration; the patient is going through normal states of sadness, coming to terms with loss, and is now in a position to repair whatever damage or wrongdoings they have caused. Bravo!

Major Depression

Although the focus here is not on major depression, many of the same communication skills are applicable within the matrix of the borderline personality. What follows is a brief outline of major depression, described as a serious illness that affects a person's family and personal relationships, work or school life, sleeping and eating habits, and general health.

Major depressive disorder (also known as clinical depression, unipolar depression, or unipolar disorder) is a mental disorder characterized by an all-encompassing low mood accompanied by low self-esteem and loss of interest or pleasure in normally enjoyable activities. The term *major depressive disorder* was selected by the American Psychiatric Association to designate this symptom cluster as a mood disorder in the 1980 version of the *Diagnostic and Statistical Manual of Mental Disorders* (DSM-III) classification, and since has become widely used. The diagnosis of major depressive disorder is based on the patient's ability to cope. People who suffer with clinical (chemical) depression find they have little, if any, control over their emotions and moods.

Therapists can assume there will not be much changeability from one session to the next. If the patient was blue when he came in last week, he will be the same patient when he comes in this week and the following week. Most common are morbid stories, negative thinking, self-blame, and regrets for past shortcomings or wrongdoings (self-hatred turned inward). In severe cases, depressed people may have symptoms of psychosis. But even though they may not be hallucinating, they imagine and predict unpleasant or catastrophic happenings that are not reality-based (e.g., *Chicken Little*, "The sky is falling!"). Many are hypochondriacs; at the least sign of an illness, they immediately plan for their demise. Because these patients feel so psychologically suffocated, they commonly complain of fatigue, headaches, difficulty breathing, bodily pain, digestive problems, and such. Other symptoms of depression include loss of appetite, withdrawal from social situations (friends, families, and colleagues), diminished sex drive, and sometimes thoughts of death or suicide.

The depressed patients at the more severe end of the spectrum (those who have attempted suicide or have suicidal tendencies) may require extensive hospitalization, along with psychopharmacological treatment with antide-pressant medication and mood stabilizers. In essence, for our purposes of communication, can we say that BPD is a shame disorder while the depres-sive borderline has a guilt disorder?

The Depleted Depressive

Although they may have many similarities with those who are experienc-ing major depression, the most pervasive characteristic of the depressive borderline is reflected by their object relational bond, mainly bonding via the *Mother of Pain* through victimization, persecutory anxiety, and self-hatred. These are the borderlines who not only *feel* the pain or the paraly-sis; they *become* the pain or the paralysis (undifferentiated state). This is almost a reverse narcissist, a person so depleted of external supplies that they resort to pain and victimization through parasitic dependency. To communicate with the depressed borderline the therapist must help them get in contact with "real needs" and speak to the sadness and the losses, not to the depression.

Communication style and technique are similar for those in both the depressive and the major depression states. Therapists must first address:

- How one not only feels depressed but becomes the depression (a psy-chotic moment). "No wonder you feel paralyzed. There is a difference between *feeling* depressed and *becoming* the depression."
- How one feels under siege. "I can imagine how badly you feel when oth-ers complain and attack you, but you are the one who is most attack-ing" (harsh, punitive superego).
- How one confuses depression with loss and sadness. Depression is pathological sadness, and dealing with sadness and loss is a sign of being mentally healthy. "No, you are not depressed; you are dealing with loss. This is a healthy state of mind. Before when you were manic and all over the place, you thought that was healthy."

Case of Wendy

I Am My Depression!   The following case is another example that illustrates how the depressive borderline not only feels depressed, negative, and rejected, but actually becomes the depression, the negativity, the isolation. The depressed borderline may feel sad, stuck, and paralyzed, and the case also shows how patients confuse a state of paralysis with actual paralysis. This is very much like a psychotic patient who cannot distinguish inner belief from outer realities. Homage is due here to Fairbairn, whose major contribution was to distinguish the state of being from the state of doing: "I feel; therefore, I am."

> *I feel cold; therefore, I become the coldness—an iceberg.*
> *I feel scared; therefore, I become the scary monster.*
> *I feel hungry; therefore, I become the hunger (eat everything. in sight).*

Wendy (W): We have been in a relationship for five years. He promised me the world, marriage, children, and a home. I am now 40 years old, and my fertile years are passing by.

Therapist (Th): But you are also saying he doesn't follow through on the little things either—like the time he promised to take you to the jazz quartet and the time he promised to take you away for the weekend.

W: I guess you're right. I overlook a lot.

Th: Interesting how you saw some danger signs early on but overlooked them.

W: I did see them. I just feel so desperate that no man would ever want to be with me.

Th: Desperate?

W: I am very depressed, feel very sad and blue when alone, and need a man in my life.

Th: Being depressed is not the same as feeling sad.

W: What's the difference?

Th: First tell me why you feel "depressed?"

W: My father was an alcoholic, and my mother was never available. She ran a rooming house to make extra money and completely ignored me and my little brother. She slept with various men just to be able to support us but was never there for us.

Th: So, you are talking about very early losses.

W: I felt that my sister and I were a big burden to her, and if it weren't for us she wouldn't have been put in that position.

Th: So you feel guilty for being born and getting in her way.

W: I guess.

Th: Wendy, this is very important—what you are telling us—because none of this was your fault. You were not responsible for your mother's fate. Besides, she had choices. She could have chosen other ways to make a living. You have never really mourned the loss of your father, or dealt with the guilt, a burden you carry for your mother.

W: Guess not.

Th: Your mother is the one who should feel guilty, not you. What you need to do is recognize the difference between feeling sad and being in a depression. You have everything going for you career-wise and otherwise.

W: I still don't understand.

Th: If you feel bad inside, this will make you feel desperate and unattractive and contribute to choosing men who are unavailable. You are deserving of much more.

W: But I don't feel as though I am.

Th: I know. That is why we are having this discussion. Those are not feelings; they are defenses (internal rejecter).

W: I never thought of it that way. In a way that makes me feel better.

Th: Right. Because now you are in control as opposed to being a doormat that just sits and waits for someone to "show" up, who from the onset is unavailable.

This case illustrates how primitive defenses in the paranoid–schizoid position impact the ability to see reality. What contributes to Wendy's depressive borderline state is her involvement with unavailable men and a defective ego that is not able to recognize red flags from the onset. Wendy is object-wanting but never object-attaining—the search for the unavailable man. In treatment, she pushes the therapist away, reenacting the drama of the unwanted child. The unavailable man (or woman) syndrome is a very common symptom in situations when there has been early object loss. Unable to mourn the loss, one remains forever attached to it and recreates the loss again and again—thus, perpetuating the depression and not yet having the ability to enter into the depressive position.

Summary

Although this chapter discusses variation in depressive disorders, the main focus was on the depressive borderline, distinguishing major depression from normal states of mourning and sadness, as defined by Melanie Klein. Most common in the depressive borderline are morbid stories, negative thinking, self-blame, and regrets for past shortcomings or wrongdoings (self-hatred turned inward). Unlike the borderline who fears abandonment, rejection, and losses, people with depression are more concerned about guilt and that they will be punished (get sick, die, lose money, and end up bankrupt).

In the next chapter, we turn our attention to the obsessive–compulsive borderline, a rigid personality type who is obsessed with order and cleanliness.

6

The Obsessive–
Compulsive Borderline

*How to talk to an obsessive–compulsive? Repeat the same thing again
and again.*

Traditionally, obsessive–compulsive mechanisms can be traced to early child-hood. To paraphrase Klein (1975), if the mother is too strict about cleanli-ness, especially during toilet training years, the child develops destructive fantasies about his/her own body parts. To assuage this anxiety, the child learns to control his/her sphincter muscles and finds a way to release his/her feces in a systematic, organized fashion so as not to "dirty," destroy, or harm his external objects. To guard against this, the child learns to control others, while at the same time being careful not to "mess up." Freud refers to this process as "undoing," a way of making reparation in order to eradicate the dirt or badness. In society, these obsessive–compulsive borderlines are actually high-functioning and often extremely accomplished and successful people, including doctors, lawyers, and scientists.

Many clinicians attest that obsessive–compulsive disorder (OCD) belongs in its own category and not within the matrix of the borderline disorder or other disorders. It has been included here because, although there is an overlap in characteristics and defenses with other types of borderlines, those with OCD exhibit marked distinctions. For example, while the narcissist is obsessed with his/her sense of importance and self-worth and will do any-thing to achieve fame, success, power, or beauty, the OCD will do anything to fight for his cause, his authority, or to prove that he is right, clean, orderly, and perfect. The main distinction is in the way each type of personality expe-riences dependency needs. While the narcissist may succumb to feelings of weakness and vulnerability, the OCD fears contamination by the needs and emotions of others.

Therefore, I have tentatively moved them into the "Land of Borderville," not only because they are stuck with their compulsions, but because they share a grandiose self that infects and invades other disorders. The grandiose omnipotent self trespasses into both narcissistic and borderline territory and plants its fertile seeds. "I am Mr. Perfect, and I have come here to put order into your life." Taking into account these differences opens up an entirely new dimension in how we "talk" to an OCD as compared to how we "talk" to another type of borderline or even a narcissist. For example, the narcissist tags the self with the badge of entitlement (all the attention, all the fame, all the time, all the money), whereas the OCD could care less about attention and is more concerned with domination/control, saving, hoarding, order, and cleanliness. Unlike the narcissist, OCD personalities are consumed by objects and addictions. They are the collectors, the pack rats, the savers, and the withholders, and feel entitled to put others on hold while they wash, clean, inspect, check, and recheck. Needs, feelings, and emotions are experienced as dirt or filth, so they spend their lives hiding from the shame of these "dirty" little interjects. In essence, their obsessions over their objects become the replacement for love and intimacy.

A glaring example of this overlap is seen in the Nazi Party leader, Adolf Hitler. Driven by his narcissistic grandiosity and omnipotence, he was led to the fantasy that he could conquer the world and obliterate an entire culture of Jews. Could we say he was borderline in that he was racked with anger and rage from a traumatic childhood? Or was it from his OCD obsession, as Peter Loewenberg (1987) reminds us, to get rid of all the "dirty Jews" and cleanse Germany as a representation of his own "dirty" internal self? "I, your leader, will save you from contamination!"

Diagnostic Features

According to the *Diagnostic and Statistical Manual on Disorders* (DMV-IV; APA, 1994, 304.1), the obsessive–compulsive personality is distinguished by a preoccupation with orderliness, rigidity, perfectionism, and power/domination over interpersonal contacts at the expense of flexibility and spontaneity. OCD types are characterized by a chronic preoccupation with cleanliness, orderliness, and control. Degrees of this disorder range from mild to more severe. When these behaviors become disabling, they impact others around them. For example, in a social setting or when things are not done to their liking, the OCD individual may either withdraw or become very hostile. "Who told the hostess to put salad dressing on the salad? Doesn't she know better?" The individual usually expresses affection in a highly controlled or stilted fashion, but is very uncomfortable in the presence of others who are emotionally expressive. The person often has difficulty expressing tender feelings and rarely pays compliments.

> *It was so humiliating. We were at my best friend's wedding when suddenly I heard this loud, uncontrollable voice yell out, "Hey, what's the matter with you all? The music is too loud! Would you turn down that G-d awful noise?"*

OCD Qualities

- Dysfunctionality (inability to trust judgment, perception, reality testing; distortions in thinking)
- Primitive defenses (splitting, projection, projective identification)
- Characteristics/behaviors: controlling, domineering, tyrannical
- False self (pretends to be caring/fatherly/authority figure)
- Grandiose/omnipotent self (the world should wait for him while he cleans, checks, and counts)

Pack Rats and Hoarders

One of the most puzzling and taxing borderlines is the OCD borderline hoarder. This is the type of person who hoards and collects electrical gadgets such as wiring, computers, disks, and has a garage full of broken drives, radios, and televisions. According to Kobrin (2010), the hoarder is linked to people with Asperger's Syndrome, who find ways of communicating their isolations and detachments from the world through hoarding. The high-functioning Aspergers are often accomplished physicians, linguists, engineers, accountants, etc.

In terms of communication, it is important to recognize the differences and similarities between other types of borderline personality disorders and OCD borderline disorder. To make this distinction clear, in this section I will use the term *BPD* for all types of borderlines other than those with OCD. Both BPD and OCD involve individuals with severe attachment disorders.

Patients with BPD are more inclined to overtly take revenge and attack their objects through envy, fear of loss, attachment to objects, and terror of separation. Both have difficulty trusting their reality. "Did I lock the door? I must check again and again." Both the BPD and the OCD are fixated in a fusion with the early mother, a maternal object of attachment and disturbance. The OCD is obsessed with fear that if things are not exactly perfect, orderly, and spotless, something terrible will happen, whereas the borderline's obsession is with separation and fear of abandonment. These unconscious conflicts in both disorders keep repeating in the effort to overcome early deficits. Those with BPD have even more striking similarities to OCD patients. Both have difficulties in ego regulation, and both operate at the level of the paranoid–schizoid position and part-object functioning. Prevalent in both BPD and OCD are such primitive defenses as splitting, projection, and projective identification, ego deficiencies, as well as the inability to trust reality, perception, and logical thought and reasoning. "If I wash my hands 50 times a day, I will remain safe. If I am sick, suicidal, or bleeding, he/she will not leave me!" Both BPD and OCD individuals feel persecuted by their needs. The OCD experiences internal emotions and sexual intimacy as dirt and filth to be eradicated. The outside world is a dangerous place for them. The OCD fears that enemies will contaminate them by injecting emotions and demands into their holy, germ-free land. For the BPD, the enemy is the one who exacerbates an already existing anxiety of abandonment.

The OCD, like the borderline, exhibits a false self. Under the guise of a good cause, being a protector or savior, he/she will elicit suffering and humiliation in the other. The OCD demands complete dominance, is anal, and seems to be an all-knowing or all-encompassing authority figure, whereas the borderline acts out emotions ranging from revenge to victimization.

The narcissist displays his omnipotence by shattering his objects' sense of being, self-identity, or self-worth, as if they do not exist. This can be devastating to the borderline partner, who already has a thwarted sense of self (Lachkar, 2002). Both the narcissist and the OCD are the masters of pain, especially emotional pain and abuse. Similar to those with OCD, narcissists will withdraw or withhold time, money, sex, and attention. Both have hidden agendas to humiliate their partners. "Oh, my husband was much too busy to celebrate our anniversary; he said he would do it another time, as if to say our marriage has very little significance. He is an 'everything' and I am a 'nothing'!"

Following is the case of Mr. X, a high-powered attorney whose focus was completely on perfectionism.

The Lawyer and His Briefs

Mr. X. came into therapy at his wife's insistence that if he did not seek treatment she would divorce him. She told him that she was fed up with their marriage and could not deal with his aloofness, coldness, preoccupation, and criticism of her and their kids. The trigger was the rage and anger she felt when her husband kept her and the kids waiting to go on a family vacation. He instructed her to pack and be in the car by 8 a.m. "We didn't leave until dark. I should have just gotten out of the car with the kids and cancelled the whole trip, but then he could care less, for he has no emotions. He would have just gone back in to write more briefs. That's all he does: keep people waiting!"

Therapist (Th): Hello! I am glad you were able to make it!

    Mr. X: Sorry I'm late but I had to be sure I had my briefcase, my keys, and all my notes for court.

    Th: Well, we don't have too much time left, but we will do the best we can, and maybe next time you can leave a bit earlier.

    Mr. X: No, it's not the traffic. You see my wife is lazy and very emotional. I am the one that has to check the house to make sure the lights are out, the doors are locked, that the dog has water.

    Th: So, the responsibility is all in your hands.

    Mr. X: Well, if I don't do it, she certainly won't.

    Th: But you have three kids, and so far she has taken good care of them and hasn't burned the house down.

    Mr. X: You don't understand. She is too emotional. She is always crying, whining, making demands. All she wants to do is talk about "feelings."

    Th: Feelings?

    Mr. X: Yes, feelings. I am not an emotional guy. I admit it. I just want her to be more efficient and when she sees a piece of paper on the floor to pick it up.

    Th: Don't you think the floor will survive if she doesn't do it right away?

    Mr. X: No, you do not get it.

    Th: Mr. X, we can talk about paper on the floor, lights, locks, or files, but then we are not going to be able to deal with the reason you are here, and I know you like to be brief.

    Mr. X: You're right. Why am I here?

Th: You are here because your wife feels you don't love her and that you are cold and distant.

Mr. X: She's right. I don't like all that emotional stuff.

Th: But you are not married to a light bulb. You are married to a woman—a woman with feelings and emotions who would like to express her love for you.

Mr. X: She is more than emotional; she is hysterical. She yells and screams! That's when I would rather be talking to a lamp. My mother was always calm and cool. She would never allow us (siblings) to get out of control or out of hand. Everything in her house was perfect and spotless.

Th: Ah, is that where you are confused?

Mr. X: Me confused? I am a top lawyer in my firm, and everyone thinks I do the greatest briefs.

Th: Your wife also says the same about you. But she told me that the last few times you wrote such amazing briefs you were late for court and the judge postponed the trial.

Mr. X: That happens a lot. I lose track of time and get so involved with the briefs that I forget I'm running late, and then, in addition, I have to check the house before I leave.

Th: Did it ever occur to you that by being so perfect you become imperfect (opening the space for the "language of dialectics")?

Mr. X: You may be right. I did not care so much about winning the case. I was more concerned about writing a perfect brief.

Th: You think you are a perfect husband by making sure the house is safe, but you have another house that has been very much neglected: your internal emotional house that you have locked yourself out of.

Mr. X: I know what you are getting at.

Th: Yes, your emotional side has been locked inside, and I believe you are here so we can open up that space.

Mr. X: But I find emotions and feelings to be dirty and disgusting. Who would want to open up that can of worms?

Th: Worms? Dirt? Hmmmmm. Mr. X, I believe you are confusing a man's healthy emotional side with dirt and filth. Your emotions are your treasures. Just a little while ago you told me that you didn't care about your client having his case postponed because you were too busy writing the perfect brief.

That is the "dirty" part, where you disregard other people like your wife. But your emotions—those are pure and real.

Mr. X: Maybe I worry that if I allow myself to express emotions I will sound like my hysterical wife.

Th: Excellent point, and I see where the mix-up is. Your idea of expressing emotions is when someone yells, screams, or whines. That is acting out. Expressing emotions has to do with words, like you and I are doing right now. I think you feel you only have two choices: (1) to sound like a histrionic out-of-control wife, or (2) to be like a cold, emotionless, spotless mother, with no feelings or emotions.

Mr. X: (Tearful) I feel so ashamed and sad, but I don't want to lose my wife, and I have to confess that even people at my firm are beginning to complain that I can't keep up because I take too long. My assistants say that I constantly correct them and am overly critical.

Th: Ashamed!? What you call shame, I call progress: that you can face this imperfect part of yourself. Of course, you love your wife and family and, if you allow me to be brief, this is the healthy part of you!

Mr. X: Thank you.

Th: A pleasure! See you next week.

Mr. X is clearly a homegrown OCD. But he is also a composite of many features of narcissism and other borderline disorders. He is narcissistic in the way he feels entitled to keep people waiting, in his obsession with perfection, and his lack of consideration, empathy, or concern for others (e.g., keeping the wife and kids on hold while he writes his briefs and interrogatories). Even though he fits the diagnosis of an OCD, he exhibits his borderline side in the way he loses his boundaries, intrudes into the space of others, and is unable to observe his behavior and how it impacts others (ego dysfunctionality).

The Dance of the Obsessive–Compulsive Borderline

Obsessive–compulsive people typically choose an opposite type as an object choice. These types include histrionic personalities, as well as those who are dependent, unorganized, messy, sexually exploitive, and loud. They are often provocative, flirtatious, and will do anything for attention. One wonders why these two oppositional types stay together. In the dance, they meet each other's unconscious needs. For the OCD, it is the emotional part long ago abandoned or never claimed. For the histrionic, this represents order and structure in a messy, unorganized, dysfunctional world. The more the OCD withholds attention, love, and emotion, the more hysterical, emotional, and needy the partner becomes. This needy and demanding self exacerbates the disgusted and emotional part of the OCD that equates needs, dependency, and feelings of vulnerability with dirt and filth. Emotions mess up his orderly, compartmentalized world and create chaos and vulnerability. The most pressing problem for the partners of OCDs is how to handle the insecurities and abandonment anxieties the OCD's coldness, aloofness, and unavailability stir up in them.

The Sadistic OCD

This chapter would not be complete without a discussion of the sadistic obsessive–compulsive. In the sadistic OCD, all the elements of internal dirt now come to the forefront. The sadistic OCD does not have a well-integrated superego marked with normal morals and codes, but instead has a persecutory and sadistic superego that usually runs amok with his/her obsessions. Sadistic OCDs are closely aligned with the malignant borderline but differ in being more driven in their planning and plotting. They are cruel, violent, and evil, similar to the malignant borderline but less impulsive. In addition, they reach for "higher" goals—i.e., to humiliate, demean, and exterminate an entire race. The main objective is not to inflict pain—although this can be a secondary gain—but to establish dominance and do anything to fight for a higher cause.

"Now I am free to expose and express my dirty little boy self. I can eat blood, piss, or expose excrement. Now I am in control of my feces, not my mother!" The bitter paradox of the OCD is that the very dirt they try to avoid is the dirt they create.

Case of Judy and Francois

Therapist (Th): Greetings! Who would like to start?

    Judy (J): I would, because I wrote Francois a letter telling him how much I love him, and when he is himself and his defenses are down he is the best. I wrote to him because when I try to talk to him he belittles me or tells me I'm crazy and too emotional. I wrote that I know he loves me and our family, and is invested in keeping our family together. But he must listen to me and pay attention to my needs.

Th: So, writing a letter was like an insurance policy that you would be heard.

J: Right. The last time I tried to tell Francois how I was feeling he disregarded what I said.

Th: So, Francois, you disregard Judy in the same way your father disregarded you?

Francois (F): My father was terrible. I was a very sensitive kid. I wanted to be an artist. He would laugh, poke fun, and say the best thing for me was to be a technician.

Th: I totally understand how devastated you must have felt when your father vehemently deprived you of your artistic endeavors and reduced your artistic ambitions to the level of a technician.

F: When he said that, I stormed into my room, locked the door. And you know what he did?

Th: What?

F: He broke the door down and beat the crap out of me.

J: Francois had a terrible childhood, a terrible father. His mother committed suicide. I had a wonderful family, and to this day I thank them. I remember that right before my father died Francois promised we would get a little condo on the beach. When I reminded him of his promise, he shrugged his shoulders, laughed, and said, "You forget I have a boat, and the boat needs to be updated." I am so angry! I'm sick of him and his boat!

Th: Francois, why do you think your needs are more important than Judy's or the family's?

J: Pardon me for interrupting. He acts under the pretense that the boat is good for the family. He does not even participate in family activities with our son (skiing, tennis, and soccer) unless we all go out on the boat!

Th: Francois, so now you are letting us know that your deprived childhood was so devastating you have to let your wife and son know what that feels like—an enactment of the childhood you never had. Andrei is a child and needs a father, but it is hard to be a father when no one was available as a father to you.

F: He was a bully, not a father!

J: My son would love to have his daddy ski with us. He says daddy doesn't like to ski or do anything with us.

F: It is hard for me to do things with them because they get very messy. I prefer to go on my boat, clean it, and organize it.

Th: You can't stand a mess?

F: No! I can't stand the sloppy way she puts the books on the bookshelves and gets mad when I try to fix them. I am an artist. I have a very creative eye. I can't stand to see things out of order.

Th: You can't stand to see things out of order because you think this is the way to clean up a messy childhood.

J: That's exactly what he does. Cleans, organizes, and rearranges things. He does not even allow Andrei to play with his toys.

Th: I understand your frustration, Judy, but I also understand Francois' frustration, as well. How can he be a loving and caring husband when no one showed him love and caring, let alone how to be a parent. So now we have a little boy who wants to play to make up for the deprivation.

J: But he also does the same thing with money. Yet, I know this goes beyond money, just another way of not honoring me.

Th: Francois, I am sure your boat is beautiful and it gives you much pleasure. I wish you both a good and happy life. On the boat, you are the captain of the ship. You are in control: no messes, no emotions, no feelings. But, you are also the master of your family, to see that your family remains safe and healthy.

F: I never thought of it that way (looks over to his wife lovingly).

Th: See, that is the healthy part of you that can show emotions.

J: Thank you, Doctor!

Th: Okay, we need to stop here. See you both next week.

In the language of dialectics, Francois perpetuates the early deprivation. By depriving his wife and child, he exacerbates his deprivation even more, thus bonding to the internal mother of pain. By reducing Judy to a low-level wife with no entitlements, he makes her into a mechanical object, a reenactment of what his father did to him as a child. So he thinks that by being a bully he has separated from his father and is now the master; but from a psychological point of view he actually "becomes" his father.

Summary

It is not an easy task to communicate with an obsessive–compulsive borderline, for he/she often rambles on, asks one to repeat the same thing again and again to ensure they "get it right," and can keep people endlessly waiting and on hold. While the OCD is a very distinct personality, he or she does not live in a vacuum and does exhibit many borderline defenses and characteristics. Those with OCD provide us with a wonderful opportunity to make use of the language of dialectics as they display such obvious opposing dynamics. Emotions are felt to be dirty; obsessive cleaning and pickiness is regarded as cleansing, while in fact, it is the reverse!

7

The Antisocial Borderline

Individuals with antisocial personality disorder (APD) will do anything to gain money or power; they will lie, cheat, embezzle, and harm even the people closest to them. I almost hesitate sending the Antisocial Borderlines to the *Land of Borderline* for fear that they will invade and resurrect a group of victims desperately trying to heal from past emotional wounds. The antisocial borderline could enter this land with the prospect of being the savior, the healer, the giver, the caretaker, only in the end to betray and recreate the trauma and shock of the people who have been his/her victims.

In *How to Talk to a Narcissist* (Lachkar, 2008b), the antisocial narcissist was presented as one of most serious pathologies, mainly because this personality type lacks the supervisory powers that emanate from an intact superego. These personalities have no conscience, are consumed by insatiable greed, and are driven by unleashed entitlement fantasies. One woman came into the office hysterically sobbing that her husband took all her jewelry and pawned it to pay off his debts, and later was mortified to learn that her husband had forged her name and taken out all the money from their bank account. Another patient, a man who had left his wife and two kids to be with his "soul mate," was horrified when he returned home to find that all his furniture and belongings had been taken out of his house, including a valuable rare book collection.

Treatment of the antisocial borderline is somewhat limited, because not only do these personality types resist treatment, but their therapists are often repulsed by them. Moreover, they are extremely manipulative, and therapists need to be aware of their insidious and subversive behaviors. Countertransference is one thing, but far too often the therapist colludes with the antisocial borderline, who are often so "terrorizing" that even experienced therapists dissociate from the reality of what is going on in the therapy room.

The antisocial offender includes stalkers, sex offenders, child molesters, and serial killers. So in "talking" with an antisocial borderline we also need to extend our efforts to include people who have been victims of their transgressions (family members, business associates, intimate partners). The most pervasive trait of the ADP is disregard for authority, which often leads to their arrest and imprisonment. They have little regard for others and may act impulsively or plot and plan methodically how best to target their victims.

Both the antisocial narcissist and the antisocial borderline lack empathy and have no conscience, guilt, remorse, or capacity to experience concern for others. They have a grandiose sense of entitlement and omnipotence, but differ in their level of superego functioning. If the antisocial narcissist's superego could talk, it would say, "You must be rich, famous, and successful, and don't let anything stop you; beg, borrow, or steal to get what you want." Bernie Madoff was a perfect example of this mentality as he duped people into investing while he played out his grandiose ideas as both investor and consultant in his infamous Ponzi scheme. Success means one must never stop to draw a line on behavior. Insatiable greed runs amok in the case of antisocial narcissists. More! More! More! If the borderline's superego could talk, it would say, "I am your persecutory superego. I don't care about success or fame; I am out to attack, harm, get revenge, destroy, or kill (mostly figuratively but sometimes quite literally) at any cost!" I am reminded of a patient who came from a very well-to-do family; however, the mother was very withholding and stingy. "Now I shoplift for the things I was deprived of as a child, and don't care if I get caught; that will teach *her* a lesson!" This attitude is reflected in the concerns expressed by a Florida district attorney about a child molester who had finished serving his prison sentence:

> District Attorney Tony Rackauckas gave public warning about the release of child molester George England, convicted in 1977 on four counts of child molestation, including the molestation of an adopted Vietnamese girl he assaulted for eleven years, beginning when she was five years old. Rackauckas noted that the most striking aspect upon England's release was that he showed no shame or remorse. *(Orange County Register,* March 11, 2010)

An exaggerated sense of entitlement allows narcissists to deceive themselves into thinking that they are above the law and can get away with their antisocial behavior. "No one would ever arrest the son of G-D." Similarly, antisocial borderlines experience remorse only when they get caught and sometimes do not even care about that. These distinctions impact how we communicate.

To the Antisocial Narcissist:

You embezzled the money from your company because you felt entitled. Your boss did not give you a promotion, just as your father never gave you extra money to buy a bicycle. You feel badly only because you got caught. Because of your omnipotent sense of entitlement, you thought you were above the law. I know you feel badly about being caught. But for the first time, do you realize this is not all about you?

To the Antisocial Borderline:

You embezzled the money from your company not because you needed it, but because you wanted to show what it feels like to be robbed as you were robbed of your childhood. You feel badly only because you got caught, not because you believe you did something wrong. Or maybe you don't feel badly, because you feel the bad people deserved what they got! But the feeling of revenge you are experiencing is against yourself, how you betrayed yourself by disregarding your abilities. Consider this: If you can mastermind these illegal scams and devious plots, just think of how successful you could be if you put your talents to use in a legitimate way!

People with antisocial personality disorder are also referred to as sociopaths (no longer listed as a category in the *Diagnostic and Statistical Manual of Mental Disorders*, 4th Edition [DSM-IV]) and/or psychopaths. The terms *sociopath* and *psychopath* are used interchangeably, and the differences between them have become blurred. Professionals not only dispute whether there is a difference between a sociopath and a psychopath, but even among those who believe a difference exists, there is dispute over what those differences are. For our purposes, the term sociopath will be used in conjunction with nonviolent antisocial disorder, and the term psychopath will be used in conjunction with violence and perversions. What follows is the current DSM-IV Diagnostic Criteria for antisocial personality disorder.

DSM-IV-TR Diagnostic Criteria for Antisocial Personality Disorder (301.7)

There is a pervasive pattern of disregard for and violation of the rights of others, occurring since age 15 years, as indicated by three (or more) of the following:

- Fails to conform to social norms, as indicated by frequently performing illegal acts or pursuing illegal occupations.
- Deceives and manipulates others for selfish reasons, often in order to obtain money, sex, drugs, or power. This behavior may involve repeated lying, conning, or the use of false names.
- Fails to plan ahead or displays impulsive behavior, as indicated by a long succession of short-term jobs or frequent changes of address.
- Engages in repeated fights or assaults as a consequence of irritability and aggressiveness.
- Exhibits reckless disregard for safety of self or others.
- Shows a consistent pattern of irresponsible behavior, including failure to find and keep a job for a sustained length of time and refusal to pay bills or honor debts.
- Shows no evidence of sadness, regret, or remorse for actions that have hurt others.

Overlap

There is crossover between the various kinds of disorders described in this book, and certainly overlap exists between the malignant narcissist and the sociopath. The malignant/antisocial narcissist is driven mainly by the insatiable need for fame, power, and attention and disregards the needs of others for the sole purpose of self-gratification. The antisocial borderline is a closer cousin to the antisocial narcissist but more malicious. antisocial borderlines lack empathy, but they do have a conscience (an internal superego that meticulously regulates their behavior and responses from and to others). Sociopaths may be considered inflated narcissists in that they feel entitled, but with added elements of sadism and envy, as well as destructive and murderous impulses. Both the antisocial narcissist and the borderline lack empathy and manipulate or cajole to use others to fulfill their own entitlement fantasies (lie, cheat, cajole, seduce, lure). Briefly stated, while the narcissist cheats, steals, and lies to play out some omnipotent fantasy of entitlement, in general narcissists do not resort to violence. On the other hand, the borderline cheats, steals, lies, makes fun of others, and even murders for his own sadistic delight or for the sake of revenge. A sociopath is an extreme narcissist with a sadistic, jealous, vindictive dark side. Sociopaths rationalize their destructive impulses and behaviors by finding justification in seeking vengeance against "bad" people who hurt them. Unlike the narcissist, the sociopath does not experience guilt but believes that, since the world is a vicious and malicious place, there is no need to feel guilty after attacking or destroying his/her victims. According to Vaknin (2007), psychopaths are also sadistic and take pleasure in inflicting pain on their victims or in deceiving them. Some may even find this funny and amusing!

Mr. W. came in sobbing one day, saying that the FBI had finally caught up with him, and he was to be incarcerated for fraud and embezzlement. When asked how he felt about embezzling elderly people who trusted him, who put all their life savings and investments into his hands, he responded, "Oh, they are just a bunch of old fogies who will soon die anyway!" "So, you feel no remorse?" "Hell no! The only thing I feel remorse about is that I won't be able to see my kids or my wife. Believe it or not, (sobbing like a baby), I can't even look at the mailman, the gas station attendant, the clerk in the market. I am jealous of them. They are free, and I will be pent up in a prison for five years. They don't live in a huge house like mine, drive a Jaguar, wear expensive clothes, but they are happy with what they have, and they have freedom." "So you do have remorse." "Only for myself and my family, not for anyone else." "So, that is what you feel sad about: not that the children, heirs, and the elderly themselves have had their funds ripped off?" "No, that doesn't bother me in the least." "How would you feel if someone did that to you?" "That would never happen. I know every trick in the book."

Shakespeare's Iago "An Honest Man"

> "I am an honest man . . . ."

—From Shakespeare's *Othello*

Although Shakespeare never used the term *antisocial*, he must have had a clear sense of this personality type when he created Iago in his play *Othello*. "Honest" Iago is one of the most interesting of Shakespeare's characters in that he is cunning, smart, and manipulative—a master of deception. He pretends to be caring and benevolent toward others, but whatever he does is for his own self-serving purposes. Today, he would be referred to as a psychopath. In Shakespeare's day, he was called a villain. He swindled money and jewels from Rodrigo while trying to take his lover Desdemona away from him. When suspect, Iago begins improvising an amazing number of stories to cover up his lies and scams. His transgressions eventually push Othello and others toward a tragic ending, with Desdemona dying and Rodrigo wrongly sent to his death. Cassio is another character duped by Iago, unaware that all the while Iago was plotting his death, as well. Yet even when Iago confesses to Rodrigo that "I am not what I am," Rodrigo continues to trust him, as do the others. Everyone has been taken in completely by his "Honest Iago" facade.

Treatment

Unfortunately, many challenges exist when treating mentally ill patients, particularly criminal offenders. These offenders might be resistant to treatment, mental health professionals might be afraid to treat them, and the offenders might perceive the helping professionals as an extension of the justice system and not as their advocates (Lamb, Weinberger, & Gross, 1999). However, these challenges can be overcome by identifying a sound treatment philosophy and clear treatment goals. This chapter is useful for forensic psychologists and people in the criminal justice system. It also has applicability for the family, friends, spouses, partners, co-workers, and acquaintances of these offenders, who often have difficulty dealing with the guilt and shame of having been involved with such immoral people. Mentally ill offenders cause difficulty for the criminal justice system, which needs to put in place comprehensive programs based on a treatment philosophy that balances individual rights and public safety and includes clear treatment goals (Lamb, Weinberger, & Gross, 2004).

Not all people treating criminals and people with deviant behavior are analytically trained, but those who are can appreciate Melanie Klein's work (1927) and will find it invaluable. Of particular interest is her take on how criminals ward off anxiety by blocking out guilt emanating from the superego—the conscience missing in the mind of an antisocial. Klein further explains how the pathological self meets and matches the criminality of a persecutory superego only to be absorbed by an ego in harmony and synchronicity with the false self. "Nothing wrong with knocking off this guy; he deserved it!" Within the venue of the language of dialectics this offers us another opportunity to communicate with these two worlds (the false/denying/delusional self vis à vis a world of morality and values).

It is amazing how people with these pathologies, people who live in a Judeo-Christian-based society, believe they can get away with their sociopathy. Here we retrieve the "false self," mainly of the borderline, the self that belies the true self and creates an entire persona to fit the crime. These are the charmers, fixers, caretakers, all-encompassing givers, the charismatic types that can dupe even the most seasoned therapist. "Oh, Dr. Analyst, I have been to so many therapists and they were all terrible. So glad I found you. You are amazing!"

> I met the nicest guy. He was so loving and thoughtful, would take me to the nicest places, bring me gifts, flowers. And then gradually it stopped. He claimed it was because he was in debt and needed money. So I loaned him $50,000.00, which he promised to pay back. When I first mentioned getting back my money, I got the cold shoulder, silence. Every time I mentioned it later, his response kept getting more violent. He would slap me or bang me against the wall. I was afraid to call the police because then I knew I would never get my money back. Suddenly he disappeared, and I never heard from him again.

Many people are caught in this dilemma. They fear reporting the violence because, if they do, their partners may lose their capacity to work or, as in the case above, never pay back the victim. Laws should be revised to find a middle ground for dealing with antisocial borderlines that includes special workshops, anger management seminars, couples counseling, assigned monitors, and so forth.

Profile of an Extreme Antisocial Borderline

In 1978, Ted Bundy was found guilty in the murders of two Chi Omega Sorority sisters at Florida State University in Tallahassee, as well as that of Kimberly Leach. He was also charged, but not tried in a number of Northwest states, including Washington, Oregon, Utah, and Colorado, for approximately 40+ (the actual number is unknown, and Bundy took that information to the grave) murders of women from 1974 through his capture in Florida in 1978. Bundy was executed in Florida in 1989. His basic symptoms were those of an antisocial personality, with an extreme disregard for the rights of other people.

Background on Ted Bundy

Evidence of serial killers' dysfunctionality can often be tracked to incidents that occurred in early childhood. In many cases, their backgrounds reveal deviant behaviors such as cruelty to animals and small children, vandalism, as well as a fascination with knives, guns, and fire. Personally, many of these murderers outwardly appear to be immensely charming, with a persona that can fool people with their false innocence. A major clue is the absence of con-science, guilt, and loyalty to others. One patient reveals how a child would steal family silver or a neighborhood dog and sell them for a profit. Others would throw rocks or even terrorize the people closest to them or forge checks and embezzle funds from their own family members. What would a therapist do if she/he knew then what everyone knows now? What follows are some early clues and red flags concerning Ted Bundy's childhood background and some responses that a therapist might have made in retrospect.

Theodore Bundy was born on November 24, 1946, and was executed on January 24, 1989. His birth took place in a home for unwed mothers. In addi-tion to the shame of illegitimacy, Bundy grew up with a confused identity, thinking his mother was his sister and his grandfather was his father. Along the way, there were several name changes, which left Bundy with no clear identity of who he was. He was never even sure who his biological father was. When he was only three years of age, his aunt caught him smiling while arranging knives around her neck while she was napping. He also saw his grandfather (who he thought was his father) torturing animals. Bundy himself would mutilate animals, which fascinated him to no end. Bundy was a loner and, in his isola-tion, could not understand why people had attachments to one another. He was a habitual liar; he compulsively stole and shoplifted. He later claimed that he was also involved in voyeurism at a young age, specifically by peeping into windows, for which he was arrested twice. He had a girlfriend, to whom he proposed and who subsequently dumped him. Later, she accepted his proposal, and then he dumped her. After that he began his killing spree.

Melanie Klein's pioneer work in object relations provided the impetus for such concepts as infantile projections, distortions, and delusions. But her greatest contribution was the freedom and the space to express and develop a fantasy world in children. Early on, she recognized in children all kinds of sadistic fantasies and an inner drive and compulsion to express them. Klein's pioneering work in play therapy allowed children to take toy images of men, women, animals, cars, and trains, and so forth, and mutilate, cut, beat, slice, destroy them, and repeat the same hostile, sadistic acts again and again. Play therapy provided an opportunity for the child to act out fanta-sies in a controlled atmosphere, thus reassuring the child (and the parents), that it is okay to have and express these thoughts in an appropriate manner but not to enact them (Lachkar, 2008b). Klein recognized that children have the desire and impulse to destroy, cut up mommy's breasts, mutilate daddy's penis. Through play therapy the child learns the difference between the act of "doing" and the act of fantasizing about "doing" it. I believe that criminals, murderers, torturers, and terrorists have a much diminished fantasy life. They are unable to distinguish between reality and fantasy and therefore have to "do it" rather than fantasize about "doing it" (beheading victims and engaging in other bodily mutilations, severing limbs, gouging eyes, and so forth).

What would Melanie Klein do if she were alive today and had an opportunity to treat Ted Bundy? The first and foremost thing she would be likely to do is to have him sit on the floor with her and play out his fantasies with dolls and toys through play therapy. Or she might say, "I see you like to play with knives, and when you do I see you are smiling!"

Fantasy Analysis of Ted Bundy

What follows is the first of two fantasy analyses, showing how Melanie Klein might have treated a five-year-old Ted Bundy with play therapy:

> *Ted:* I don't want to see Mrs. Klein. I hate her.
>
> *Mother:* Ted, you have never met her. She is here to help us.
>
> *Ted:* I don't need any help; no one can help me. I hate everyone.
>
> *Mother:* That is why we are here.
>
> *Mrs. Klein:* Hello, Mrs. Bundy. Please come in so we can talk. Then I would like some time alone with Ted.
>
> *Mrs. Klein:* (returning later): Hi, Ted, I am Mrs. Klein.
>
> *Ted:* (Sulking and very resistant.)
>
> *Mrs. Klein:* Okay, I have talked to your mommy and she will be waiting in the waiting room while you and I play.
>
> *Ted:* (Reluctantly enters playroom filled with toys, life-like dolls representing family members, cooking equipment, play knives, stuffed animals, etc.)
>
> *Mrs. Klein:* Let's start with cooking. Here are some play knives and some play food. How about preparing dinner? (Mrs. Klein observes while Ted takes the knives and starts cutting up the mother, and later father, dolls.)
>
> *Ted:* (Smiling and slicing up the doll's breasts and genitals.)
>
> *Mrs. Klein:* Oh! I see you are very angry with mother and would like to slice her up in little pieces.
>
> *Ted:* (Continues to cut up stuffed animals. He holds one stuffed dog upside down and lets out a big sound of relief.) "Now I got you!" (He begins to laugh.)

Mrs. Klein: I see you are enjoying cutting up mommy and causing the little doggy pain.

Ted: (Big smile.)

Mrs. Klein: Your mommy has been telling me that you really enjoy playing with real knives and making animals cry and feel pain.

Ted: Yeah!

Mrs. Klein: Ted, I think you are showing the pain you feel when you are neglected and mistreated by others.

Ted: (Puts all the dolls off to one side. Takes the little boy doll [of self] and places it under a chair.)

Mrs. Klein: Now you are telling us how everyone leaves you and how alone and lonely you must feel. Because you are little you don't know how to tell people how you feel, but you are telling me about your anger with mommy and how lonely you feel away from her and the world.

Ted: (Starts to slice up the daddy doll.)

Mrs. Klein: Now you are telling me how you miss having a daddy. You are showing me that instead of missing daddy you cut him up and throw him in the trash. Because you are smiling now it makes you feel like a big boy—very powerful—and then you don't need a daddy.

Ted: I am my daddy.

Mrs. Klein: Not only are you your daddy, but you throw him away so you don't have to miss him.

Ted: But I threw him in the trash.

Mrs. Klein: You threw him in the trash because you feel he threw you in the trash. You did nicely today, Teddy. I will call your mom and we will have a chance to play again next time. Bye now.

Ted (Grunts): Bye.

Mrs. Klein: (to mother): Mrs. Bundy. At home be sure to help Teddy use his big-boy words. He is having difficulty expressing his feelings and acts them out destructively because he doesn't know how to express them. He does not seem to know right from wrong and confuses normal childhood destructive fantasies with reality. I will see you next week and meanwhile I will continue to work with Teddy to help him feel safe and eventually help him move away from his lonely, isolated world.

Second Fantasy Analysis of Ted Bundy

The second fantasy analysis describes how a therapist might treat a person who was mortified to find out that the man she worked with was a murderer. This analysis, which stresses communication, involves Ann Rule, a crime writer who worked with Ted Bundy at a suicide prevention center. She did not have a clue that the man sitting next to her was a serial killer, even though she was researching his crimes at the time. Ann Rule has since become one of the most prolific writers of high-profile crimes, authoring more than 36 books on the subject. While the actual events are real, the case is not.

Fantasy Analysis of Ann Rule

The Stranger Beside Me . . . Ted Bundy

Therapist (Th): Hi, Ann.

Ann: Well, I am in complete shock.

Th: Understandably so!

Ann: Can you imagine? Here I am, an expert on criminality and I get duped like this. All the while sitting side by side with Ted to find he was a serial killer.

Th: No clue?

Ann: No! We met in 1971 at a Seattle crisis clinic, where we both worked the night shift, answering suicide hotline calls. Who would ever believe the guy sitting on my left would end up being one of history's most notorious serial killers!

Th: You sound not just shocked but angry with yourself, as if you should have known better.

Ann: Yes, especially me. I always wanted to be a cop, but got rejected because I couldn't pass the eye test.

Th: So you feel you should have been able to "see" him for who he was.

Ann: Yes, I can't blame my eye defect for missing clues about what was going on inside Ted. That's what I am so angry with myself about.

Th: But there is something else, Ann, that you are not "seeing."

Ann: What's that?

Th: That these killers are first-class charmers, often very intelligent. They know how to bring on the charm and put on an act. Even the most seasoned therapist can be duped by them.

Ann: That makes me feel better. Can you imagine me, an aspiring cop and now a crime writer, sitting next to a serial killer, only to be awakened to the fact that he engaged in necrophilia—actually returning to the crime scene to line dead lips and eyes with makeup and all? Aren't you surprised that he went back?

Th: Not really. Often little children have fantasies about killing and mutilating; however, they learn that it is okay to fantasize but not to actually do it. Bundy was living out some murderous childhood fantasy and destroying bodies, but then wanted to put them back together again.

Ann: He was obsessed and I didn't see it. It was only later I found out that John Hinckley, who shot Ronald Reagan, and David Berkowitz, the Son of Sam killer, corresponded with Bundy when he was in prison. He was an insatiable killer.

Th: The positive outcome is the way you repair the pain you feel by writing about these killers and the triggers that stir them.

Ann: Bundy had an abusive childhood, and when he was a young paper boy he was betrayed again by a female friend. This led to the presumed murder of an 8-year-old girl on his route, who mysteriously disappeared in the middle of the night. Her body has never been found. The skimpy details available about this crime leave readers wanting to know more, offering further proof of the public's never-ending fascination with serial killers.

Th: So, in hindsight you feel that with all this data you should have picked up some sign that something was wrong with Bundy?

Ann: I guess you're right. I am being hard on myself.

Th: As tragic as this whole thing is, the outcome is positive. In addition to raising five children and doing consulting work in the criminal justice system, you have written over 36 true-crime books and have become a prolific and respected profiler of serial killers. This knowledge of and insight into extreme antisocial behavior is a gift you are giving us and helps us to sharpen our perception of the psychopathic mind.

Discussion

Not all of us are sitting next to a serial killer or have him "in our face," as was the case with Ann Rule. But the same shock and fear occurs in innocent partners who discover the person with whom they are most intimate is a liar, cheat, or a criminal. Ted Bundy may not be the homegrown jihadist who lives next door. Still, many are shocked when they discover people whom they believe would never commit a criminal act engaging in suicide bombings and blowing up buildings. In the fantasy analysis above, the therapist used a technique—which will be detailed in the last chapter, on treatment and technique—that involves "listening to the words." In this case, the word is "eye." Here the therapist uses the eye metaphor as a theme to show the two sides of Rule's situation: the eye that cannot see being transformed to the eye that saw beyond. On the one hand, the fact that Rule was blindsided by Bundy reminded her of an earlier injury (rejection when the police department did not hire her because of her poor vision); on the other hand, through her research and writing, she has peered into the events that go into the making of a serial killer and allowed her readers to see into the minds of cold-blooded killers.

The Dance of the Antisocial Borderline

Antisocial borderlines create pressing concerns in their objects. One of the most anxiety-laden and ambivalent concerns is the fear of reporting to authorities the criminal acts and violations of their antisocial partners. "He will lose his job, and then what would we do if he is in jail?" There are also the issues centering around betrayal, abandonment, self-doubt, confusion, and omnipotent denial. "Is this really happening?" In relationships, antisocial personalities often hook up with someone like narcissistic or borderline partners. The narcissists are so preoccupied with fame and fortune that they are inclined to overlook the wrongdoings of their partner, whereas the borderline may sense something is wrong but doubt their perceptions and think they are imagining things. Many narcissists stay with antisocial borderlines for secondary gains—the wealth, power, and fame. Others stay out of fear, terror, internal emptiness, and helplessness. Finally, there is the difficulty in communicating, which only leads to attack, denial, or violence. Because the borderline maintains a bond with "the mother of pain," he/she invariably destroys the joy and happiness of others. In treatment, the therapist resorts to the special language of dialectics, talking to the stranger within and the stranger without.

Summary

As Freud reminds us, "aggression feeds upon aggression." Domestic violence does not occur all at once. It is insidious, starting slowly with subtly hostile remarks and verbal abuse and gradually but inevitably escalating into random violence (slapping, slamming doors, uttering threats).

There are many variations on the theme of the antisocial personality. But what we can abstract are the common traits of a "con artist." With their well-developed persona, cleverly disguised false self, excellent verbal skills, and charming personalities, antisocials can dupe even the most seasoned therapist, and the armor of charm they wear makes it easy to fool their innocent and unsuspecting victims. Applying the language of dialectics, one must address two sides of the conflict: (1) the capacity for growth and reparation, and (2) the resistance to change and need to maintain a persistent bond with bad internal objects (the mother of pain, betrayal, abandonment).

> *Just think of the intelligence and brilliance it took to mastermind this scheme/scam and plot this embezzlement. With your magnificent mind, you could have developed your own economic empire. But apparently revenge was more important than success and your potential achievements. So while you are here we have an opportunity to make reparation to those who have been damaged.*

The antisocial leaves behind a trail of victims who are mortified and traumatized by the damage done to them. Treating and communicating with the victims of these perpetrators involves soothing them and letting them know that they are not responsible for staying or working with, or being otherwise linked to these criminals. Often individuals are horrified and mystified by the shift and sudden turnabout of mood and behavior on the part of the antisocial borderline who, for no apparent reason, suddenly terminates a relationship, quits treatment or a job, or just moves away and is nowhere to be found again. The nonsuspecting innocent victims are often in shock to hear that the person they trusted is being tried for theft, drugs, fraud, sexual offenses, or other criminal acts. The worst is yet to come: the antisocial partner does not even care! Their victims should not be surprised to wake up one day and find a stranger in their beds.

8

The Passive–Aggressive Borderline
"Promises, Promises!"

Introduction

In *How to Talk to a Narcissist* (Lachkar, 2008b), the passive–aggressive narcissist was presented as one who feels entitled, who feigns illness or helplessness to coerce others to perform his/her functions. The passive–aggressive borderline also coerces others to take on responsibilities, not so much because of a feeling of entitlement but because the passive–aggressive borderline is oppositional. They are the "imaginary invalids." Both the passive–aggressive narcissist and the passive–aggressive borderline share a grandiose self in that they expect others to be responsible and do things for them and pick up their covert, nonverbal messages. Both have a subversive way of evoking rage in their objects since they cannot express anger, which drives their partners and the people who know and work with them to frustration. Both are victims of traumatic childhoods, so they believe that the world owes them something and that people should take pity on them.

They do, however, have their own idiosyncratic differences in the way they experience entitlement. The passive–aggressive narcissist, for example, uses, misuses, and abuses his/her objects because of feeling entitled. For example, a passive–aggressive narcissist was late to the theater and explained to the manager that he lost his keys, could not find his ticket or a place to park, and expected to be seated without waiting for the intermission. The passive–aggressive borderline, on the other hand, uses objects of entitlement in reverse. Their entitlement fantasies center on their oppositional nature as they covertly coerce others to feel sorry for them by feigning helplessness and pretending to be powerless. "I really didn't want to go to the theater, so I lost the tickets. I just can't understand why my husband got so pissed!" Thus, while both may share the same symptoms, they are driven by different end goals and motivations. For the borderline, the drive is twofold. First, they are addicted to the mother of pain (illness, accidents, forgetfulness), and second, they bond with the unconditional caretaker who oversees them—a re-creation of the parent–child dyad. These distinctions are of fundamental importance as we prepare communication approaches most suitable for the passive–aggressive borderline.

The passive–aggressive borderline differs from the mainstream borderline. The most notable distinction between these two is that mainstream borderlines allow themselves the full range of emotions—expressions of rage, anger, revenge—whereas the passive–aggressive borderline conceals and fails to express his/her rage.

A Portrait of the Passive–Aggressive Borderline

The passive–aggressive borderline personality is marked by such traits as helplessness, procrastination, parasitic dependency needs, forgetfulness, and a passive attitude toward social or interpersonal relations and occupational situations. The personality traits of the passive–aggressive borderline are marked by a pervasive pattern of oppositional and negative attitudes. This is not an easy disorder to describe, because there are many variations on the theme. Some passive–aggressives are very meek and mild, whereas others are outwardly negativistic, defiant, and intrusive. The first type is the manipulator, who coerces others to do things for him or her. Therapists are often duped by the mild and meek manner in which these borderlines present themselves. They frequently convince others that they suffer abuse from society, their jobs, their marriages. They judiciously and unconsciously persuade others to take pity on them. Because many passive–aggressives are victims of traumatic childhoods, they induce and produce conciliatory responses. "Look! I'm all black and blue. I had to go to work at that dumb job, but I hit my head on the car door!" Passive–aggressives are notoriously klutzy; they fall, have accidents, and get ill frequently.

The term *negativistic* is not quite suitable for many passive–aggressive borderlines, who truly believe they are good and compliant and feel that others are the ones who are nasty and have negative attitudes. Many people who deal with these personalities are deceived by their innocent persona. Even therapists are completely baffled about how and why their "innocent" patients are being so mistreated by society, only to find out later how the passive–aggressive borderline frustrates and provokes others through subversive behaviors. "Sorry, I'm late again. I had to make some important calls before coming here." At work, they defy orders and resist authority figures who tell them what to do. Because of this resistance, the passive–aggressive borderline presents many treatment challenges, although there are many openings for effective communication with these personalities.

Overlap

The passive–aggressive is no longer a distinct category in the *Diagnostic and Statistical Manual of Mental Disorders* 4th Edition (DSM-IV) (APA, 1994); it is now listed as "not otherwise specified," or as an oppositional personality. However, the passive–aggressive is being considered for reentry in future revisions of the manual. Len Sperry (2006), in his revised book on personality disorders, argues that it is essential for this disorder to be reinstated. I find this category invaluable, especially in conjoint psychotherapy. Individuals with passive–aggressive personality disorder may complicate their situation with astounding laziness, compulsive eating, and reckless spending. Addicted persons with passive–aggressive disorder present a dual treatment challenge.

Signs of Passive–Aggressive Behavior

- Exhibits chronic lateness, forgetfulness, procrastination
- Makes promises that are never fulfilled
- Resents authority
- Shows parasitic dependency (cannot ask directly for help to satisfy needs)
- Acts out needs through helplessness and sickness (real or imagined)
- Coerces others to perform their tasks and duties
- Fears expressing anger directly
- Fears dependency and rejection
- Is unable to act the role of responsible mate/parent (the "baby mommy" or the "baby daddy")

- Fears intimacy at a level of maturity ("My husband—the baby")
- Creates constant chaos and confusion
- Makes excuses for tasks not done and promises not kept
- Coerces others to pity him or her; assumes role of the victim, blaming others for their own shortcomings
- Expresses envy and resentment toward those apparently more fortunate
- Expresses persistent complaints of personal hardships and adversity
- Is unaware of how his or her aura of incompetence impacts others (ego deficiency)

Treatment

Passive–aggressives are extremely difficult to treat because they always try to recreate the parent–child dyad. They feel trapped and paralyzed by their dependency needs and act out their victimized selves via their dysfunctionalities. They wear their partners out to the point of exhaustion, until finally the caretaker partner caves in. They drive their partners insane because they are the procrastinators, the big promisers, and the do-it-laters. The most dominant feature is an unbearable repressed hostility and anger that stem from a deprived or neglected childhood characterized by caretakers who were inattentive to their needs. Passive–aggressives are the couch-potato husbands and wives; the forgetful ones. "Anger in our family was simply verboten. My German father would slap the hell out of us and say, 'Now you have something to cry about.'"

The kind of treatment approaches suitable for the passive–aggressive borderline include psychodynamic, supportive, cognitive, behavioral, and coaching. In this chapter the emphasis is on communication that focuses on the importance and privilege of allowing emotions to be expressed directly and freely.

The Dance of the Passive–Aggressive Borderline

A common trait in passive–aggressive borderlines is a disregard for authority, which often leads to arrest and imprisonment. Since these personalities have little or no regard for others, they may act impulsively or plot and plan methodically how best to target their victims. The types of pressures they instill in others are mainly feelings of rage, anger, and confusion.

Passive–aggressives are the silent terrorists and are very taxing on the therapist's empathy because they are like slippery fish: the minute they are caught, they offer a barrage of excuses, unaware of how transparent they are. If the problem were not so severe, the passive–aggressive's behavior could be quite comical. For example, an aerospace engineer claims he missed his appointment because he could not find his socks. Another patient, a certified public accountant, was three months behind in his payments because he ran out of checks. Therapists need to be aware of the passive–aggressive's extreme dependency and manipulative nature and of their ominous and rebellious conduct. Any person who deals with them—even a therapist—can be in a perfectly fine mood when suddenly a swell of uncontrollable rage seeps into them. "It was almost like a foreign object hitting me when I got a call from Mrs. B telling me she was going to be late again for the third time in a row because she had some 'important' phone calls to make. I suddenly felt rage burning inside of me. This is not coming from me, but must be what my patient is experiencing and does not know how to express." The dance of the passive–aggressive borderline becomes a movement between the introjective/projective processes, with the patient unconsciously translocating a split-off part of themselves onto the therapist. "I think, Mrs. B, you are telling us that you did not want to come to the session and felt that other things were more important than your mental health."

The Third Grade Teacher and Her Aide

Mrs. F: I can't take it anymore. I have a classroom of 40 third graders in a lower economic area, and because of the district I teach in, they give us an aide.

Therapist (Th): Sounds reasonable.

Mrs. F: Actually, she is more work and problems than all the kids put together. When I ask her to pass out the folders, she gives me a look of scorn. I can tell she resents whenever I tell her to do something.

Th: What a model for the kids!

Mrs. F: You got it. How do I expect the kids to respect me when she undermines everything I ask her to do?

Th: Have you discussed this with the principal?

Mrs. F: Are you kidding? I have texted, faxed, e-mailed, called her, met with her, and all she says is, "Give the aide a chance." I am ready to explode!! How many chances can I give her? She just doesn't get it. The other day we were going on a field trip, and the bus driver told the kids that under no circumstances could they eat on the bus. Do you know what she did? She passed out cookies! Guess who gets in trouble?

Th: She is a very hostile, angry person and knows how to stir up trouble, doesn't she?

Mrs. F: You bet! I don't even like the person I've become. I am constantly so angry, I could scream. She'll be standing right next to the reading books, and if I need one she doesn't budge. I then have to leave my group to go over and get the book. Finally, I blew. I yelled and screamed at her and called her an idiot. This is when everything blew. I got summoned to the office for name calling, and she gets away with her ridiculous behaviors. They think she's a nice calm person and I am a tyrant!

Th: The principle does not understand about passive–aggressive disorders, does she? And how they project their rage onto those around them, making them the angry and ineffective ones, while they stand idly by.

Mrs. F: Boy, you got that one right. But what do I do?

Th: Before we talk about what to do, first we need to discuss how she projects onto you her repressed rage, making you the angry one. Of course I have never seen her or diagnosed her. But, based on what you are saying, this is not your rage.

Mrs. F: Then whose is it?

Th: It is hers! It is her rage that she puts into you. You were in a fine mood until she started acting out. So having said that, let's talk about how to communicate with someone like that.

Mrs. F: Okay, I'm ready!

Th: First, recognize that this is not your rage. It does not belong to you; it belongs to her and gets transported to you via her projections. You at least are the healthy one and can express your anger directly; she has to stir you up to justify hers.

Mrs. F: Okay. Then what?

Th: Try and find a moment when she gets stirred up and really angry and then compliment and praise her.

Mrs. F: Compliment and praise her? Have you lost your mind!

Th: I know it sounds strange, but this is the only disorder that when the person expresses anger directly, rather than through a circuitous route, we react positively.

Mrs. F: I get it. It makes sense. Actually, I could do that with some of the kids in my class.

Th: Yes, you can, but be careful. Some aggression in children should not be encouraged. In the case of your aide—it gets high marks.

The Wife in Waiting

Th: Mrs. W, please come in.

Mrs. W: I still want to wait for my husband. He says he is on his way.

Th: It is a quarter past the hour. I suggest you come in so we can get started.

Mrs. W: Okay, I know he will come at the last minute; he always does. I don't know what to do. He is always late. He expects me to wait and wait, and I am really pissed and tired of it.

Th: This is exhausting.

Mrs. W: Not only that, I also work, have two small kids, and he expects me to do all the shopping and taking care of the kids while he watches sports, lying on the couch.

Th: It's good that you're here. You can't go on like this.

Mrs. W: I know, but what am I to do? When he goes to the market, he comes back with excuses: the market was closed and he couldn't find another market, the market was out of diapers, the credit card didn't work. I am so pissed and so angry I could scream!

Th: I hear you.

Mrs. W: It is like having another kid. I was the eldest of five siblings. I was the anointed one to take care of my baby brother while my mother tried to run the house and take care of the other kids. My father abandoned my mother for another woman, so I had no choice but to be the little mother.

Th: So you really got robbed of a childhood. You were a little girl who grew up much too early—a little adult.

Mrs. W: Exactly.

Th: So, as angry as you are, you see that this is a very familiar role. You are the caretaker, and your husband is the little baby brother that you must care for.

Mrs. W: I do see that and I'm sick of it. I'm tired and exhausted. Even when I try to nap for a few moments he starts to tickle the baby so she will wake up. Or when I ask him to hand me a bottle, he just stands there like a lamp.

Th: What was his childhood like?

Mrs. W: His father dumped his mother and got remarried. My husband was never accepting of his stepmother and kept yelling, shouting, and calling her names. His father punished him severely. He beat my husband and told him never, ever again to talk back. No one ever taught him how to express feelings, so he learned to suppress them. What should I do with my anger? I feel like exploding.

Th: First of all, the anger you are experiencing actually is not your anger! It belongs to your husband. He is projecting his rage onto you, setting you up to be the angry one so he does not have to express his emotions directly.

Mrs. W: Oh, that's great. What do I do with that piece of information? I am still pissed as hell.

Th: It is important because it will help you communicate.

Mrs. W: I do communicate. I tell him what to do, and he just doesn't do it! And then he accuses me of being a nag. Nag! Nag! Nag!

Th: See, this is a setup. He coerces you into being the nagging mother, and you play right into it.

Mrs. W: Any advice?

Th: Yes!

Mrs. W: Okay?

Th: Stop enabling him. If he goes to the market to buy diapers and the market is closed, there will be no diapers. Start with small things that you can follow up with—like if he does this again you will take away his shoes or take away the TV. Do something that will make him directly angry. What to do will be your decision.

Mrs. W: Actually I like that. I feel a bit empowered. But isn't that manipulative?

Th: What you may call manipulative, I call changing the dynamics.

Mrs. W: You're right. Better to do that than feel so powerless.

Th: That's right. He has not only stripped you of your power but has put the helpless part of himself into you. Let him know there will be a consequence. Now he will be the angry one!

Then wait for the finale—the final moment. He will be the one to blow! You then applaud. Bravo! This is the healthy part of HIM that can finally express his anger directly. So not only are we weaning him from his silent abuse, we are weaning you away from a lifelong caretaking role that no longer works.

Mrs. W: This is getting really interesting. I will get him off the couch.

Th: Maybe he belongs on this couch here. By the way, the light went on. Your husband has arrived, but we have to stop. See you next week.

Summary

In our clinical practices, we see many cases of occupational abuse, whereby an employee in a subservient position acts out his or her most hostile impulses. This was described in the first case with the aide and the schoolteacher. In the second case, the passive–aggressive is prescripted and preprogrammed to play the role of the "baby husband." Being a lifelong caretaker, Mrs. W. makes the perfect target/container for her husband's silent aggression and abuse. His brutality is often covert and insidious, which makes it difficult for others to understand why they react to him as they do. In the case of the schoolteacher, the therapist is seen as taking a very active and supportive role. The therapist exhibits an understanding of group psychology—how certain groups have the proclivity to find a scapegoat, a victim on whom they project their inhibited feelings. This is very similar to what happens in primitive cultures, described in Chapter 10: the group needs to find an enemy to project all their badness into (Freud, 1921/1979).

Even though the therapist has not diagnosed the provocateurs described in the vignettes, based on the given descriptions they seem to fit the diagnostic category of passive–aggressive borderlines as outlined in this book. It is important to mention that the diagnosis is only tentative, but until we get more information or until something more suitable comes along we take the liberty of working with what we have. The main point, although it may sound manipulative, is to bring about a situation in which the passive–aggressive can begin to experience his/her own rage. By asking the wife to think of things that she can do to "set her husband up," the therapist is right on track. Changing the dynamics alleviates the wife's stress because she will no longer be swallowing and internalizing all her husband's rage. This is how the therapist helps the patient to seize the moment and embrace the shift in dynamics. The language of dialectics reaches its zenith when the therapist helps the passive–aggressive acknowledge that direct communication is far better than delivering messages in a second-hand manner. The passive–aggressive's seductive quality and victimized state make it easy for the therapist to collude with him/her, but not pointing out the "silent" aggression runs the risk of the aggression escalating and putting the caretaker-partner in further danger.

The passive–aggressive borderline is one of the most difficult personalities to treat, as well as one of the most stressful on those who live, love, and work with them. Unlike with any other disorder, we actually try to bring out their rage. This is a preemptive strike designed to frustrate the passive–aggressive borderline and transform him or her from the silent communicator to one who finally has a voice.

We now move on to a different inhabitant of "Borderville," the histrionic borderline.

The Histrionic Borderline

The histrionic borderline is someone who cries easily, has excessive parasitic dependency needs, and displays emotionality on his or her sleeve. In some instances, the histrionic borderline may appear very narcissistic. However, although they use their powers seductively, they do not necessarily do this to feel special. Rather, it is a way of provocatively bonding with their objects. Histrionic borderlines are close cousins to the dependent personality types, who typically assume that others will take responsibility for them and make up for their maladaptive ways, dysfunctionality, lack of self-confidence, low self-esteem, and inability to make decisions. The histrionic borderline will feign sickness, weakness, and incompetence and will sob, plead, and resort to anything to get people to adhere to his/her whims.

> *Why do I always get stuck with the same kind of men . . . men who only want me and use me for sex? I had a dream that I was at a party wearing nothing but my Victoria Secret underwear, and all these men came into this old, worn-out house. They started to flirt with the hostess, who was dowdy, matronly, and unattractive. I tried to get their attention, but no matter how hard I tried, they would just look away and ignore me.*

How the Histrionic Differs From Other Borderlines

The main difficulties in the treatment of the histrionic borderline is recognizing the distinctions between the dependent borderline and those with histrionic features. Dependent borderlines may resort to sickness, psychosomatic illness, and suicide threats as a way of bonding with their objects and are less concerned with being the center of attention (Giovacchini, 1993). On the other hand, histrionic borderlines rely more on emotional outbursts or threats and use their enticing qualities with the objective of maintaining center stage. Another close cousin to the histrionic borderline is the histrionic narcissist (Lachkar, 2008b), Both are similar in that they need to be the focus of attention wherever they are and use their beauty and sexual allurements to achieve their goals. But they differ in that the histrionic borderline is more likely to go into victimized states—for example, suicide threats, attacks against the self, and so forth.

Diagnostic Criteria (DSM-IV, Appendix B)

Histrionic Personality Disorder   The *Diagnostic and Statistical Manual of Mental Disorders*, 4th Edition, Text Revision (DSM-IV-TR), describes the histrionic as presenting a pattern of excessive emotionality and attention seeking starting in early adulthood, as indicated by the following:

- Uncomfortable in situations in which he or she is not the center of attention.
- Interaction with others is often characterized by inappropriate sexuality, seductive or provocative behavior.
- Displays rapidly shifting and shallow expression of emotions.
- Consistently uses physical appearance to draw attention to oneself.
- Style of speech is excessively impressionistic and lacking in detail.
- Self-dramatization, theatricality, and exaggerated expression of emotion.
- Suggestibility (e.g., easily influenced by others or circumstances).
- Considers relationships to be more intimate than they really are.

The DSM defines *depressive personality disorder* as a "pervasive pattern of depressive cognitions and behaviors beginning by early adulthood and present in a variety of contexts, as indicated by five (or more) of the following:"

- Moods dominated by dejection, gloominess, cheerlessness, joylessness, unhappiness
- Self-concept centering around beliefs of inadequacy, worthlessness, and low self-esteem
- Overly critical, blaming, and derogatory toward self
- Constant brooding, worry over future and potential disaster
- Critical, negative, and judgmental towards others
- Pessimistic

I think I first became aware of the histrionic personality because of my Polish/German immigrant mother, who would go into a total histrionic episode when I would not eat. She would first start with screaming, yelling, and threatening and then, when all else failed, would feign sickness. I remember coming back into the kitchen and finding her lying on the floor, pretending that she had had a heart attack. She would be groaning, "Oy, gevalt" or "Shrayen gevalt,"* which is how someone might respond if they were in mortal danger). It did not take long to catch on to her act. Little did I know I would be writing about this years later in one of my books.

Kernberg (1992) viewed patients with predominantly histrionic traits as having an infantile personality disorder that is closely aligned to characteristics of borderline personality disorder—mainly the flare-ups of rage superimposed with depression. The histrionic presents a perfect example of projective identification. When in the moment and when they are the center of attention, they will be clingy and act unduly helpless, dependent, and vulnerable. However, when they feel their sexual or seductive powers no longer have an influence, they feel depleted and empty. This creates guilt in the other partner, who will withdraw.

Thus the dance begins. The more the borderline attacks and demands, the more the partner withdraws, creating the very thing the borderline fears—abandonment. Their antics remind me of opera scenes in which a lover betrays a woman and she ends up either committing suicide or actually falling down, fainting, staggering, begging, and pleading for him not to leave her. Kernberg also describes men as having histrionic patterns, but they are most likely to present as the Don Juans, with the exception that their preoccupation has more to do with dominance and control over women and less about clingy dependency.

The Don Juan syndrome fits perfectly with the "as if" personality, which Winnicott (1965) refers to as the "false self," a pseudo self that belies or masks the true self (1965). Because borderlines lack a "real self," they must resort to an imaginary one to prevent the sensation of emptiness. The Don Juans are perfect examples of how borderlines operate through their seductive charm and charisma. They promise and then let down. Their inflated rhetoric and

---

* The literal meaning of the Yiddish word *gevalt* (or *gevald,* as it sometimes appears) is "force" or "violence." But the expression "*Oy, gevalt!*" (or just plain "*Gevalt!*") is similar to "Oh, my God!" or "Good grief" when uttered after something unfortunate has happened—you have just locked your car keys in the car, or your dinner partner has spilled wine all over you. Another Yiddish expression, *shrayen gevalt,* "to scream *gevalt,*" means to call for help, although it can also have the semihumorous sense of "to scream bloody murder." (*Gey shray gevalt,* "Go scream *gevalt,*" is the equivalent of "Tell it to the judge" or "Go do something about it.") When uttered in a tone of genuine alarm, "*Gevalt!*" is a cry for rescue in serious situations, like when your house is on fire.

undeniable charm can make even the most emotionally attuned observer initially believe in them.

> *I feel so stupid! How could I ever have fallen for a guy like that? When I first met him, he was so charming. He seemed so sincere. He made me feel as though I was the most beautiful woman in the world. "You are the sexiest woman I have ever met." He would call me five and six times a day just to tell me he loved me. Shortly thereafter I was in a bistro for lunch, and there he was—drinking wine with another woman, kissing and kissing her—kisses that were interminable—just as he did with me. I couldn't believe my eyes.*

> *Another woman told a man she was dating that she loved chamber music and he boasted about how much he enjoyed it, too, and said he went to concerts often. During the first concert they attended together, he fell asleep for a while, obviously not as enthralled with the music as his date was. Her suspicions that he was lying about his classical music expertise were confirmed when after the first movement ended, he started to applaud wildly, obviously having no clue that one does not clap between movements.*

In addition to weeping almost on cue, the histrionic borderline has a low level of tolerance for frustration and will not take kindly to waiting for an appointment, waiting for an answer, or waiting for gratification. The histrionic is also excessively emotional and unable to process his or her feelings. Thus, this type of borderline is characterized by severe emotional instability and frequent hysterical outbursts that he or she cannot control. According to Kernberg (1992), histrionic types are prone to emotional crises, but they have the capacity to make a quick recovery, and their clinging dependency is confined to their sexuality and ability to lure others to do their bidding. While they cry easily, they have good cognitive abilities. In my experience, especially having a practice in Los Angeles, many histrionic personalities are successful artists and actors.

A good example of the histrionic's use of allurement was graphically demonstrated in the infamously seductive birthday song that Marilyn Monroe sang to the then President of the United States, John F. Kennedy, during a nationally televised celebration of his 34th birthday. The actress flaunted her curvaceous figure in a tightly fitting dress and used her whispery, sultry voice to leave little to the imagination as she intoned—or, more accurately, exhaled—"Happy Birthday, Mr. President." Her brazen, uninhibited performance stunned many and was talked about for years afterward.

In the case of Bob and Christine that appears later in this chapter, we see how Christine gains insight into she and her husband's dynamics. Bob also claims that their sexual involvements have triangular qualities and that they often choose unavailable men by which to act and reenact their abandonment issues. Marilyn Monroe seems to have had similar abandonment issues and, despite her bombshell image, also acted the part of the frightened, hapless female who required the protection and guidance of men—in her case older, father-figure males like husbands baseball player Joe DiMaggio and playwright Arthur Miller.

Histrionics are notoriously impatient and are fixated on their own needs. The short vignette below illustrates this trait:

> Mrs. Y. cannot wait. When she calls for an appointment or to ask a question, she may call three or four times in a row. When she finally does make contact, she greets the person who answers with the accusative "Where were you? I have been trying to reach you and you did not pick up." When told she will have to wait for a more appropriate time to talk to the therapist or that she can set up an appointment, she responds, "No, this cannot wait. I need an answer now! This is urgent and you should understand that!" When access continues to be denied because the therapist is with a client, this explanation is often met with some kind of over-the-top emotional response, "Well, I can see you don't care and you are just too busy for me!"

Although histrionic borderlines may appear very narcissistic, especially because they use their powers so seductively, unlike the narcissist they do not necessarily need to feel special. Rather, they use their allurements as a way of provocatively manipulating their objects to meet their demands. I am reminded of a patient who asked his secretary to pick up a birthday cake for his wife. Since his wife realized that he was not the type to pick up a birthday cake, let alone order one, she was determined to find out who did. She teased and cajoled her husband. When that did not work, she persisted and relentlessly demanded that he tell her who ordered the cake. When he still refused her demands, she pounded the table, yelled, screamed, and started to pull out her hair. Obviously, histrionics do not react well to being thwarted.

Pressures the Histrionic Borderline Places on Others

Before discussing the kinds of pressures the histrionic forces upon a mate, partner, family, friends, and work colleagues, I would like to resurrect a couple I described in one of my earlier works (Lachkar, 1992, 1997, 1998b,

2008a, 2008b), *The Obsessive–Compulsive and the Histrionic Couple*. As a marital therapist, I developed a fascination for oppositional couples, one of which was inspired by Henry Dicks in *Marital Tensions* (1967). Dicks was one of the first to describe collusive patterns in couples. In 1959, Martin and Bird brought to our attention the first dysfunctional couple, the obsessive/histrionic couple, and explained how an obsessive husband would join with a histrionic wife—or to describe it in another way, a pairing of the "lovesick" wife and the "cold-sick" husband. Since then, Sperry and Maniacci, in *The Disordered Couple* (1998), revived the obsessive/histrionic couple, claiming that this couple is now back in full swing.

The Dance

The most effective way to understand the pressure the histrionic stirs up is to view the dynamics from the perspective of the dance between these histrionic and obsessive–compulsive personality types. In the dance an obsessive–compulsive husband projects onto his histrionic wife the feeling that her needs are dirty, over the top, out of whack. He does everything he can to push her away (fear of contamination). As he pushes her away, she becomes more emotional and hysterical, and as she becomes more hysterical he withdraws even more. So, as he keeps her endlessly frustrated, she becomes more histrionic; and as she projects her emotional, "dirty" parts onto him, he becomes more anal and compulsive. She pressures him to be more emotional, and because she is so over the top he finds justification to stay in his sanitized, compartmentalized world. The more he withholds, the more hysterical she becomes.

As she becomes more hysterical, he becomes convinced that her needs are tantamount to filth and dirt. As he feels more and more disgusted, he cleans. As he cleans, she feels more neglected because she is not the center of attention. As she demands more attention and becomes more clinging, he withholds even more and becomes increasingly obsessed with order and a regimented routine. Her emotionality messes up his orderly, compartmentalized world, while his orderliness gives a false sense of security and structure to her chaotic one. It is a dance of shame and guilt. He makes her feel shame for wanting time, attention, and getting her emotional needs met, and she feels guilty for always "messing" up his methodical, systematic existence. In addition, she makes him feel guilty for not giving her more attention. The irony of this kind of coupling is that each partner wants what the other possesses. She needs "order" and structure, and he needs "emotions." The case that follows is designed to illustrate these points.

Case of Bob and Christine

Bob is an attorney, who is married to Christine, a part-time actress. In this example, I refer to a very common type of couple—the obsessive–compulsive and the lovesick wife, the histrionic.

Th (Therapist): Greetings! What brings you here!

Christine (C): I feel as though I want to jump through my skin. My husband claims I am too needy, too demanding, and far too emotional.

Bob (B): It is not just that. She just doesn't stop. She just keeps pulling at me, touching me when she knows I don't want to be touched.

Th: But isn't that what couples do: touch, hug, kiss, and show affection?

B: The way she does it makes me sick. After a night with her I just want to wash her away.

C: That's what he does. He is constantly organizing, filing, putting things away, and washing his hands. He's like a lawyer even in the bedroom.

Th: And then what happens?

B: That's when she loses it, starts to attack me, screams, makes demands, pushes, pulls out her hair, throws herself on me as if I want to have sex with her, when that is the last thing on my mind. She even threatens to jump out of the car.

C: I do everything I can to make him feel attracted to me. I wear sexy clothes, put on mesh panty hose, wear gorgeous lingerie, and he doesn't even notice.

Th: So, even when you entice your husband, he does not notice you and puts his work and obsession first.

C: Yes, and that's when I lose it.

B: "Lose it" isn't the word. She goes ballistic. She yells, screams, tears off her clothes and throws them at me. She is just too emotional.

Th: What you call emotional has nothing to do with feelings. These are defense mechanisms, emotional outbursts based on lack of impulse control. But you, Bob, seem to have a thing about being emotional.

B: Well, I certainly don't want to act like Christine. She disgusts me when she gets like that. And she thinks this is sexy.

Th: So, you have an idea that emotions are dirty, and because your wife gets hysterical you confuse all normal, healthy expression of feelings with being dirty.

C: His mother was like that. When he was a child she always told him not to cry, not to show feelings. She even followed him around the house and made sure everything was perfect. She never kissed him or showed him any affection, and when he tried to hug her she put him down. All she did was praise him for being a good student. He's a great lawyer!

Th: Well, I do think there is some confusion here. Christine, when you feel rejected by Bob, you don't become emotional; you get hysterical. You get out of control. When this happens it exacerbates his mother's attitude that emotions are messy and dirty. And when Bob withdraws you become even more hysterical. Bob, you stay with Christine because she owns a disavowed part of yourself long ago abandoned—the emotionally split-off part of yourself. Christine, Bob owns a part of you, part of you that could use more discipline and control over your emotions, especially when you feel your feminine allure waning and are afraid that you no longer have the seductive powers you once had.

B: You're right. I may confuse dirt with feelings, but she confuses sexuality and seduction with love. She doesn't love me; she just wants to seduce me to prove to herself she is the center of the universe.

Th: You nailed it, Bob. Spot on! So while we are here, Christine, you have a chance to get more in contact with your feelings of love for Bob, as opposed to being his seducer. And, Bob, you have to learn to function as a husband. You should not keep rejecting Christine, because when you do, things turn into a mess, and then it will require a lot of treatment time to clean up the mess.

C: Thank you. This has been very helpful.

Th: Good. Take care until next time. Nice work!

Discussion

This case illustrates how to deal with the partners by using the language of dialectics, which allows us to get into the "dance" of the couple. We have an opportunity to see how Christine's exhibitionism, clinginess, and excessive dependency needs cause the direct opposite effect on others than she intends. Through the introjective/projective process, each partner projects a disavowed part of himself or herself onto the other. Within the collusive bond of this couple we have an opportunity to see the kinds of pressures a histrionic places upon his/her partner.

Treatment Techniques

- Show the dialectics between inner and outer feelings (seduction versus true emotions). In the case of Christine, we see how the outer self is exhibitionistic, a false self which belies and covers the true self, the self that can feel and express emotion.
- Show how the out-of-control enactments are not an expression of feelings but rather defense mechanisms. Many therapists confuse acts of anger or frustration as an expression of "feelings." It is imperative that the patient realize these outbursts are defenses. When the patient says, "This is how I feel," the therapist must reply, "Those are NOT feelings; they are defenses."
- Show and demonstrate how to express real feelings and stress that they are the real treasures that should be shared with others. Many patients cover up their true feelings because they feel persecuted or because something stirs their V-spot, making them feel very vulnerable. The therapist should let the patient know that their feelings are their internal jewels, that without acknowledging them they cannot develop and will remain developmentally stuck.
- Show how needing and craving to be the center of attention actually has the opposite effect of turning people away. Many patients, especially narcissists and histrionics, think that being the center of attention gives them a sense of specialness or importance. Because of a defective ego, they fail to see how this can not only be a burden to others but a turn-off. The goal in treatment is to help these suffering individuals develop better object relations.
- Show how the very thing the histrionic fears is the very thing the histrionic creates (rejection and abandonment). Many histrionic and borderline patients delude themselves into thinking that the more they cling, feign illness, desperation, or form other kinds of parasitic attachments, people will feel sorry for them, care for them, and not ever leave them. In the "real" world, this has the opposite affect. Therapists must be very

careful to communicate to the histrionic that it is not their needs that cause rejection and pain, it is their "poor-me" attitudes—the victim role they project onto their partners.

Summary

Communicating with a histrionic borderline definitely requires a different set of language tools in order to delve beyond the seductive methods the histrionic uses to allure their objects in order to uncover their real emotions. Histrionics delude themselves into thinking that they are expressing emotions, but in reality they are merely acting defensively, aggressively, and impulsively. Their true emotions are buried deep within their psyches, and their exhibitionism is a pathetic attempt at denying this. On a precautionary note, many therapists think that because histrionics act out so passionately these patients are "expressing" themselves when, in fact, these actions are defensive maneuvers designed to manipulate and lure their objects. The therapeutic task is to wean histrionics away from these aggressive, uncontrollable impulses that result when their "V-spot" gets activated and uncover the real feelings masked by their outward personas.

10

The Cross-Cultural Borderline

Sixteen ways to say "No" in Japanese.

—**Peter Berton (1995, 2001)**

Introduction

In this chapter, we venture from the confines of the consultation room moving from the domestic to the global to examine where psychopathology and cross culture meet within the context of the borderline personality. This chapter presents many challenges. The main one is to determine if there is such an entity as a cultural borderline. To do so, I feel obligated to provide some background material; otherwise our delineation will appear as wild speculation and stereotypical assessment. This brings up the question, do we have the right to diagnose and analyze an entire group of people and put them into a category, let alone on a foreign analyst's couch?

For an answer, I turn to psychohistory, which provides us with justification for analyzing a group of people by studying the group's religion, ideology, mythology, childrearing practices, and the kinds of leaders they identify with. In other words, we find validity by analyzing the group's collective myths and fantasies, very much in the same way an analyst analyzes a patient's dream. Since the world faces new challenges and surges of aggression from terrorists and terrorist organizations, it seems paramount that we attempt to delve deeper into this kind of aggression. In an earlier paper, "The Psychopathology of Terrorism" (Lachkar, 2006), I speculate that terrorists may share many traits with the borderline personality, along with characteristics and qualities inherent within the borderline structure (severe early trauma, abuse, abandonment betrayal).

Cultural borderlines not only bring to their countries and relationships a certain nationalistic pride, but also their relentless beliefs to which they vehemently adhere. They also try to persuade, if not force, others to become "believers." Those who do not comply become the betrayers or the "infidels." I remember attending a conference on women and the Middle East. After the main speaker's presentation, we broke up into small workshops. Suddenly the discussion of women's rights escalated, and the scholarly Egyptian women started bashing us, the Western women, maintaining that we were abused in our culture, which is one that thrives on greed, sex, and materialism and, instead of traditions and values, has high divorce rates and a lack of family bonds. The Western women started to bash back, stating how the Muslim women had no voice and tolerated abuse, mistreatment, torture, subservience, and obedience to men.

So, what happens when someone from another culture enters Western civilization? With them comes not only their national flag, but also an entire array of cultural traditions and customs. In relationships, adaptation plays a key role in the ability to tolerate the other partner's cultural, political, or religious views. How does this fit with the Cultural Borderline?

Psychodynamics and Cross Culture

The dynamics involved in treating cross-cultural borderline (similar to the cross-cultural narcissist as described in *How to Talk to a Narcissist* (Lachkar, 2008b), take on an entirely different shape. What shame means to a Westerner may not be what it means to a Middle Easterner or Asian. It is not enough to understand shame without encompassing the concept of "saving face" in Asian and Middle Eastern societies. Furthermore, to understand the concept of "self," one must take into account the differences between an "individual self" and a "group self." The same holds true for guilt, envy, jealousy, "true self" and "false self ("tatamae" and "honne"). One must also be aware of familial hierarchical positions that occur in many cultures, in which deference to elders and parents comes first, with wives last on the list. For Koreans, it is insufficient to analyze someone's anger or rage without considering the Korean concept of "Han" ("rage") with its deep historical significance. What dependency means in Japanese cultures is in sharp contrast to what dependency represents for the Westerner (Doi, 1973; Johnson,

1993). Consider the intense mother–child bonding relationship, known in Japan as "amae."

Subjective Experience of Culture

Where do cross-cultural borderlines fit in the Land of Borderville? Does this imply that people from various cultural persuasions are pathological? This brings up another question: Where do culture and pathology lie, and is Western psychology applicable to non-Western cultures? One man's freedom fighter is another man's terrorist. Further research is needed in this area; however, for our purposes, I take the position that violence, terrorism, and aggression are forms of pathology. In *How to Talk to a Narcissist* (Lachkar, 2008b), I distinguish between the cultural narcissist and the cultural borderline. For example, the cultural narcissist might say, "There is no other country like Italy, Mexico, Germany, Israel, Iran! I am an Italian. I'm a Zionist! There is no other place like my country! Germany is our Fatherland. Israel is our Motherland! Allah is our Prophet and there is no other God!" The borderline might say, "I will destroy anyone who challenges my beliefs from my country." The main difference is that the narcissist will identify with the country because of specialness or special identity, whereas the borderline cares less about "specialness" but more about revenge, retaliation, and vengeance against anyone who threatens or defies their country. "Don't you ever talk about my country like that again!" What follows is an example of how one culture experiences "honor," as depicted in the film *The Stoning of Soraya M.* (2008).

This film is a true story of one of the most severe forms of punishment to victims in the Muslim world. It is about a victim named Soraya who gets stoned after being falsely accused of infidelity. Her husband, who is trying to get out of the marriage in order to marry a 14-year-old girl, stages this manipulative plot to achieve his end without having the burden of supporting two families. He convinces Soraya to cook for a widowed friend and then accuses her of being an adulteress, bringing false shame and dishonor. At the end, we see her buried to the waist with only her face and head covering showing and then being stoned to death while all the villagers look on. Soraya's own father and sons were the first to throw the stones to guard the family's "honor." This brings us to another point: How do we find and justify such pathology, and how much is abnormal and how much is mentally healthy? Again, to examine these issues we turn to psychohistory.

Psychohistory and Pathology

Drawing from my work as a psychohistorian, which applies to psychoanalysis, history, political psychology, anthropology, child-rearing practices, religion, and mythology, we learn more about the etiology of these patients from various cultural and ethnic backgrounds. I believe psychohistory answers such questions as: How can human beings commit heinous crimes against their own mothers and offspring or behave in ways so foreign to us as Western therapists? Many scholars in the various fields encompassed by psychohistory are rather hostile to psychohistorians, claiming they make wild speculations and that their stereotypical assessments are subjective and invalid.

Paradoxically Freud was one of the first to write "Freud for Historians" (Gay, 1988, pp. 8–9). I cannot believe Freud's intention was so grandiose that he intended to replace history with psychoanalysis; rather, he wanted to enhance our understanding of history. He seemed to have a grasp on how unresolved childhood trauma weaves its way into the culture and affects politics, creativity, and growth (unresolved oedipal aspects of regressed sex and aggression). Today an increasing number of people in all disciplines are beginning to embrace psychoanalysis as a tool to provide deeper understanding of such things as wars, suicide bombings, enslavement, torture, human rights abuses, and issues involving the equality of women.

What is it that makes honor more important than life itself? I believe the answer lies in psychohistory. The discussion of the cross-cultural borderline is not merely based on treating a few individuals or couples and making a diagnosis involving a mere handful of patients. It encompasses a much larger vision (Gay, 1988, pp. 8–9).

Endleman (1989) in *Love and Sex in Twelve Cultures* claims that from a transcultural perspective people have vast cultural and psychological differences, that we do not share the same instinctual drives concerning sex, aggression, and oedipal conflicts. He also describes culture from without, attesting to the idea that these conflicts are not idiosyncratic but have universal application. In other words, Endleman argues that every culture strives to master and overcome its oedipal rivals. The latter is in accordance with child developmental studies and research that all human beings go through specific developmental phases, moving gradually from early basic dependency/bonding attachment with the mother to phases of separation–individuation that are inherent in every human being (Mahler, 1975).

I subscribe to the notion that the Western concept of human development holds universal and traditional concepts applicable to all human beings. Other than in the United States and some European and South American countries, I have not seen many infant/child development studies documented. Societies or religious groups who adhere to such primitive defenses as shame/blame, envy, control, domination, violence, splitting, projection, projective identification, and omnipotent denial cannot find healthy ways to deal with conflict or aggression. Instead, they hide under the pretense of religion or culture to find justification for their unleashed, unprocessed rage.

Is There a Cultural V-Spot?

In my earlier works, I described one of the earliest areas of vulnerability occurring in the Middle East. First, the myth of the Jews as "God's Chosen People" provided an entire religious/cultural group with a collective diagnosis of narcissism, while the Arabs, as the abandoned/orphaned children, garnered a collective borderline diagnosis. Stemming from these mythic origins and oedipal rivalry are age-old sentiments, passions, and feelings that continually resurface, giving rise to many collective group-fantasies. If there is such a thing as a cultural "V-spot" or collective archaic injury, one might suggest that Isaac was the narcissistic, entitled child given the birthright, whereas Ishmael, who was sent off to the desert, became the abandoned child, victimized by his fate. So, Jews got the "good breast," the land of Milk and Honey, whereas the Arabs got the "bad breast," the dry, barren one, leaving both groups in a state of endless rivalry and unsolvable conflicts. Could we say that the Arabs have never reconciled or come to terms with loss or mourned for what they felt was their inherent entitlement?

Another example of a cultural V-spot was the caricature of Mohammad depicted in a Danish cartoon. The cartoonist stirred up such an uproar that free-press publishers around the world received endless death threats. This brings up another area of controversy: Can we say that there is such a thing as a national character? Some scholars question the very concept of national character. To be sure, not all members of a given group behave in a manner consistent with that of the overwhelming majority. And some members might actually behave in a manner that is quite the opposite of the majority's "norm."

Still, one must grapple with some broad generalizations, even though we are aware of their limitations. However, is it fair to classify followers of Islam as a shame society; Germans, as a larger Christian community, as a guilt society; and Russians, because of years of KGB looking over their shoulders, as a paranoid society? One Russian patient revealed that, even living in America, "Wherever I go, I still look over my left shoulder to see if I am being followed."

Equally broadly, we might classify the Japanese as belonging to the "shame culture" (Berton, 2001; Lachkar, 2008b). Imai (1981) and Berton (1995, 2001) have written extensively on Japanese negotiating behavior, indicating that the Japanese have 16 ways to avoid saying "no." In order to avoid conflict and maintain a sense of harmony (*wa*), the Japanese are reluctant to say "no" (a form of indirectness in communications, as well as a desire not to offend). To say "no" is felt to be too directing, abrupt, and ultimately impolite. Japanese communication is usually quite loose in logical connections. One can go on talking gracefully for hours without coming to the point. That is why it is sometimes extremely difficult to communicate, especially in business matters (Doi, quoted in Berton, 1995). Much of Japanese communication is based on nonverbal expression (*haragei*), so as to not offend or hurt.

So whether or not these cultural distinctions are precise descriptions or generalizations based on the country's history and culture, these concepts provide a basis from which a therapist trained in the West can achieve a better sense of how to communicate with patients from various cultures. In essence, there is a "dance" between the cultures, but there is also a dance between their psychodynamics (shame, guilt, paranoia, etc.). Another method of understanding national character is to get a sense of the types of leaders people identify with (e.g., benevolent, weak, passive, tyrannical).

An Orphan Society: Identifying With Traumatized Leaders

Since my main focus has been on the Middle East, I make reference to Arab leaders as way of an example. It was astonishing to me to see how many leaders in the Muslim world share many of the states, traits, and characteristics common in Borderline Personality Disorder, mainly the abandoned orphan syndrome. Ranging from Ishmael to the Prophet Mohammed, it is striking how many leaders were abandoned or orphaned and how many experienced traumatic, abusive childhoods. Saddam Hussein and Arafat are prime examples of children who were raised by violent caretakers after the loss or death of a parent. Bin Laden, for example, was one of 15 children by one of 10 wives, and had another 35 siblings from his father's other wives. This is similar to what many Arab youths in polygamist societies experience. There are many children, and the father is perceived as unavailable. The absent father syndrome is a very common theme in Middle Eastern culture.

The Koran makes many references to orphans. Many leaders in the Muslim world have been orphaned. The Prophet Mohammad himself was an orphan, as were many leaders in the Muslim world including Yasser Arafat and Saddam Hussein, both of whom had very traumatic childhoods. It is therefore easy for innocent Muslims to readily identify with powerful leaders who offer the group fantasy of being the "good daddy," the messiah or messianic savior to a group of abandoned screaming babies.

The abandonment aspects are particularly significant in terms of understanding how many abandoned babies in the Arab world find compensation in bonding or forming an identification with leaders who not only concretize the mythology but also perpetuate the conflict. Al Qaeda terrorist Zacarias Moussaoui presents a perfect profile for the upbringing of a terrorist. His mother was undernourished and physically and emotionally ill while he was in utero. His father was a violent alcoholic who abused the family and finally abandoned them (*Los Angeles Times,* 2006).

Another prime example is Saddam Hussein al-Tikriti, who was born April 18, 1937, in a village of mud-brick huts outside Tikrit, a backwater north of Baghdad. Biographers describe Hussein's parents as dirt-poor farmers. Others say he was a member of the "petit bourgeois." Hussein's father is said to have died before his birth. Saddam was not wanted by his mother. He was then raised by a terrorist uncle. His mother rejected him at birth and farmed him out to others to care for him. Saddam was never breast-fed by his mother, grew up with severe maternal deprivation, and adopted the posture of "myself against the world." His mother remarried. His earliest influence was with his Uncle Khagrallah Tulfah, an army officer stripped of rank by the British after he joined a failed 1941 coup. Because he had no father, Hussein apparently formed an intense identification with his uncle and tried to please him. Taking the 10-year old Hussein to Baghdad, the older man became his guide through the political maelstrom of postwar Iraq. According to the same reporter, Tulfah had definite theories about Iraqi society, and he made them part of the boy's political education. Later, Tulfah expounded on them in a pamphlet, "Three Whom God Should Not Have Created: Persians, Jews and Flies."

Treatment and Treatment Techniques

In one of my earlier contributions (Lachkar, 2008b), I developed the concept of the cross-cultural hook as a means to find pathology within one's own culture. For example, an American wife married to a Japanese man complains that he is cheap, and does not believe in our materialistic society. In reality, it is quite the opposite: Japan happens to be hub of materialism, and invests a great deal in shopping and, of course, technology. In fact, objects often become the replacement for human contact. Another way to examine culture is through the leaders with which the group identifies, the child-rearing practices, and the treatment of women.

Treating individuals or couples from another culture can be overwhelming and cause much frustration, not only because therapists may not have an understanding of their languages, traditions, childrearing practices, or identities, but because some of the resistance and rigidity to change or adaptation to their current environment is so embedded in these patients. In terms of treatment, I refer to five basic points:

1. Finding the cross-cultural hook
2. Reversing the scenario
3. Replicating something familiar
4. Learning a few basic words in the patient's language
5. Using countertransference

The cross-cultural hook is a "diagnostic" tool I devised to aid in treatment (Lachkar, 2008b). This technique pinpoints pathology by spotting contradiction or hypocrisy within one's own culture. For example, a Japanese wife finds solace in nursing her baby while sleeping with the baby in another room. She states that this is a common practice in her culture. The therapist then has an opportunity to point out the contradiction. "But it is also a tradition in your culture for women to please their husbands and make them come first." What follows is a case of a Middle Eastern man married to an American woman.

Natalie and Abu Omar

Natalie, an American woman, is married to Abu Omar, who was born in Baghdad. They have been married for five years and have a three-year-old child. The presenting problem centers on the role of the wife. Who comes first: the wife or the mother?

Therapist (Th): Salam (therapist greets the couple in Arabic and starts to shake hands but notices that Abu Omar pulls away).

Abu Omar (AO): Salam (Hello).

Th: Please have a seat and we shall begin. So, I would like to hear from each of you what brings you here. Who would like to start?

Natalie (N): I will start.

AO: No, I will start.

Th: Very well.

AO: My wife does not understand my culture, that in our relationship my mother comes first. To me my mother is the most important person in the world. We had a conflict: My mother had a big celebration with family, and people came in from Baghdad especially to be with us. I told my wife that she had to stay at home with the baby.

Th: So, she was not invited?

N: No, I was . . . (interrupted by Abu Omar).

AO: Please. I am not finished (aggressive tone). So I went to my mother's, and when I returned Natalie was very angry and upset.

Th: Natalie, can you respond and tell us what your view is?

N: Well, this is what he always does. He puts his mother before me, and whenever I complain he says that it is traditional in his culture that mother comes before wife.

Th: Well, I guess you are here to see a therapist trained with Western values to help sort out this area of "culture clash."

AO: Yes, I would like that.

Th: The confusion lies within the differences between our cultures. In our culture, the wife comes first. She is considered first and foremost, as she is also the mother of your child.

N: That is exactly what I try to tell him, but I feel he only uses this "cultural stuff" to suit his own self-serving purposes.

Th: Oh, what do you mean?

N: Well, he acts like a true and faithful Muslim, but will step out of his tradition when it suits him. When he lived in Baghdad, he frequented a night club on the outskirts. He had a woman there, and he locked her in her room, went out on the town, drank liquor, did not pray, and ate pork. Yet he claims to be a devout Muslim when he says his mother comes first. So where is his tradition?

Th: Natalie, are you saying that Abu Omar is using his tradition as a tool to keep you subservient?

AO: Hey, wait a minute. This is not why we came here. I did not come here for you to shame or dishonor me.

Th: Abu Omar, this is another cultural clash; in our country trying to understand something is not the equivalent of shame. In no way am I judging you, I am here to help you have a better, more harmonious relationship with your wife, and I gather this is why you are here.

N: Exactly!

Th: Natalie, I give you a lot of credit to point out the contradiction that maybe the therapeutic issues are not so much about who comes first, but rather how you feel you aren't being treated the way your husband is capable of treating you.

AO: No, I treat her very well.

Th: Your going to your mother's celebration without Natalie would be like if you came to one of our meetings of women, and I locked you in a room until the meeting was over, saying it was our tradition. That would not make you feel very good.

N: What a great example.

Th: Even though it is great example, it still does not undermine the difficulty and struggle for Abu Omar to adapt to our ways, which are still very foreign to him (showing empathy toward his plight).

In the above example, the therapist uses the language of dialectics to show what would happen if the situation was reversed, and Abu Omar was the one being "locked out." Note the use of the word "Salam" to say hello and goodbye. The use of a few simple words in the patient's language will help make him/her feel accepted and more relaxed—and that you respect and are interested in his/her culture. Be sensitive to the patient's basic customs and biases (for example, Abu Omar was not comfortable shaking hands). In the countertransference, the therapist tries not to give way to Abu's Omar's aggression, showing empathy toward Natalie and her feelings of rejection, as well as empathizing with Abu Omar's difficulty in adapting to Western cultural values.

Child-Rearing Practices

Another way of understanding culture is through understanding the culture's childrearing practices. According to deMause (1974), the roots of terrorism are inextricably linked to childrearing practices and are the result of an abundance of screaming, neglected, and abandoned orphans. He offers a chilling account of life in Islamic fundamentalist societies, which is filled with violence, cruelty, and sexual exploitation of children. These are familiar themes in countries that do not stress the importance of healthy childhood development. Even though others may refute this, one wonders how many studies on infant/child development have been done in Baghdad or Saudi Arabia.

This book holds the position that both parents are responsible for the child's development. It also holds that the Oedipus complex is universal and that all children go through similar states of development as those described by Western psychologists. Ideally, the mother provides the nurturing and protective capacity, while the father helps the child separate and individuate. In the Winnicottian sense, it is the father who provides the "holding environment" and the "transitional space" to help wean the child away from mother to the outer world (Winnicott, 1965). But if the father is absent, or if the holding environment is damaged or defected, the child's momentum to drive forward during crucial phases of the separation process becomes thwarted. In addition, the proclivity to borderline organization is greatly increased.

It is noteworthy that children raised in neglectful, abusive, traumatic environments grow up with defective bonding relations and stay forever connected to the "Mother of Pain," forming relational bonds that are destructive and painful (traumatic bonding). This takes us to the heart of the matter. As horrific as the pain is, it is preferable to a black hole (Grotstein, 1987). The emptiness is the black hole, the epicenter of the conflict. Individuals who grow up without a sense of identity turn to any idea, ideology, or belief that gives them some semblance of belonging. "At least I know I am alive. I feel excited. I have meaning and purpose to my life. Better to be an addict, a killer, a rapist, a terrorist than to vanish into the abyss!"

This fits with and is applicable to the dynamics within the cultural borderline—the concept of envy. Melanie Klein understood more than anyone the destructive nature of envy—the need to destroy the object that is most desirable, that seems most unattainable. She claims that healthy children grow up thinking that the world is a good, happy, and healthy place (the "good breast"). On the other hand, children who are raised in an environment of abuse, deprivation/privation, and abandonment grow up thinking the world is a bad, dark, dangerous, and persecutory place (the "bad breast"). This leads to splitting. One could say Allah is the good breast and Mother is the bad one.

The Workplace

These cultural dynamics are not only applicable to helping the therapist communicate with patients and couples; they are also extremely valuable to understand how these dynamics impact the workplace, institutions, universities. How about someone who says they will do it today, but really means *mañana*? In some cultures this is almost a way of life. And it is not unusual to get frustrated by a Japanese colleague, employee, or staff member who says "yes" when they really mean "no." In particular, Japanese respond more to the negative question than the answer (Berton, 2001). The Japanese will do or say anything to maintain harmony and peace (*wa*). The same holds true in the Muslim world. What we call deception they call self-protection. If a Muslim promises something, then suddenly changes his mind, they usually frame it as, "It was the will of Allah" or "Inshallah."

Summary

Communicating with a person from another culture is not an easy task, and certainly one is not expected to learn the special nuances and traditions in various cultures. However, there are a few fundamental ones that are important to know and which can be most helpful in communication. In treating the cultural borderline, it is important to understand how some people will fight to hold onto their own traditions, values, and holidays, while others may go to the other extreme and act in the opposite direction. One man of Hispanic heritage would beat his son whenever he saw him being lazy. "No one is going to tell me I have a lazy son who is going to do it mañana and be a dirty Mexican!"

Countertransference issues may become so intense that the therapist begins to feel enormous frustration and weakness in the approach to treatment. This often causes therapists to begin to feel inadequate. At this juncture, the therapist must give up the concept of "cure" and turn to mirroring as a means to reflect and empathize with the stresses and strains of adaptation. Finding the cross-cultural hook helps diagnose and determines how much is cultural and how much is pathology. On a precautionary note, remember that under the rubric of tradition, one can act out their most aggressive, heinous, and cruel impulses.

11

Final Thoughts

With these closing thoughts, I would like to restate that our visit to "Borderville" is in no way meant to be derogatory. In fact, I am delighted to welcome borderlines as they return from Borderville to a world that loves, embraces, and appreciates them for their creative talents and the unique gifts they offer. For example, many borderlines have made major contributions to society, especially in the entertainment industry and in such fields as science, literature, architecture, fashion, design, and the arts—including dance, music, and painting. Many borderlines are extremely talented, creative, and artistic. One might surmise that this is in part because of their lack of conformity, which may work in the service of their creative endeavors.

We can also appreciate borderlines' persistent desire to work through their traumatic childhoods, as well as their desire to bond with others and form healthy attachments. We cannot help thinking that if they only had experienced a "good enough childhood"—or, as Winnicott puts it, at least a "good enough mothering"—what amazing people many borderlines could have turned out to be. "I really wanted to be a violinist. I got accepted into the Julliard School of Music, but my mother thought it was a waste of time just fiddling around when I could get a 'real' job."

In these closing pages, I would like to address treatment techniques and suggestions for therapists. Many of these suggestions are also useful for parents, partners, teachers, and business colleagues who deal with borderline personalities. Crucial therapeutic functions include listening to the words, understanding the importance of humor, and using appropriate communication styles and techniques. My concept of an ideal experience is that, when patients leave a session, they leave with feelings of warmth—almost as if they have been at the theatre or musical concert. This is not so much to provide happiness as to offer them a new experience—a new space in which thoughtfulness leads to hope and understanding. The transformation of the human experience that therapy can bring about is truly an amazing process. People think they want sex, money, happiness, or excitement, but what they are really searching for is to find meaning in their lives—to make meaning out of the meaningless.

What follows are some significant therapeutic functions, which serve as useful facilitators for communication.

Treatment Points and Procedures

In discussing the language of dialectics in the treatment of borderlines, one cannot ignore the importance of basic therapeutic functions.

Crucial Therapeutic Functions

- Empathy
- Listening
- Understanding
- Introspection
- Therapist as mirroring object
- Therapist as self-object
- Therapist as container (hard object)
- Therapist as transitional object (the bonding/weaning Mommy)
- Therapist as the holding/environmental Mommy
- Therapist as the "being" versus "doing" Mommy (remembering the patient's experiences and affects)
- The cross-cultural treatment hook
- The V-spot (pinpointing the patient's deepest vulnerability)
- Humor
- Therapist as interpreter

We must not forget that our primary function as therapists is to listen closely and carefully to what the patient is—and is not—saying. Sometimes we help patients merely by providing an objective ear and encouraging them to see their situations more objectively themselves. I am reminded of a therapist in one of my supervision groups who felt guilty charging a patient because all she did was sit and listen. The group quickly made her aware of the vital importance of "listening," and that she did indeed earn her money.

Humor Is Essential

We often forget the importance of humor in the analytic or psychothera-peutic environment. Laughter is an immensely important form of commu-nication. Humor and wit are often healing for the patient, in addition to dispersing tension and gently coaxing the patient out of the status quo into more rewarding choices. In addition, therapists cannot always take to heart everything the patient says. In *How to Talk to a Narcissist* (Lachkar, 2008b), I make reference to a conference I attended on humor and psychoanalysis. An analyst told his patient that he was going on vacation. Horrified by the announcement, the patient said, "Dr. M, if you go on vacation, I will kill myself." The therapist then mockingly responded, "Oh, Mrs. S, please don't do that! At least wait until I get back." She laughed and looked at him know-ingly as if to say, "He has my number."

Humor is particularly important when dealing with borderline personali-ties, especially those who have difficulty with confrontation and interpreta-tion, those who tend to distort and hear everything as a criticism or an attack, or those who suffer from persecutory anxiety. Humor takes the edge off and transforms the behavior into something absurd and laughable rather than bad and imperfect. The therapist need not be a stand-up comedian. A smile and a few whimsical words can work wonders. One borderline patient had difficulty with separation during the weekend break and said she would like to spend the weekend here in my office, sleeping on the couch. I responded, "Great. You'll enjoy it. This is a five-star hotel!" Another patient wanted some water and saw several bottles on the table. He delicately asked if he could have one. I answered, "Sure. This is an open bar here!"

A burly, athletic, passive–aggressive patient had a great deal of difficulty getting up in the morning to go to work, yet he was obsessed with the LA Dodgers and totally idealized them. He was captivated by their diligence and endless perseverance. "Wow! I'm glad you don't play with the Dodgers," I commented. "Can you imagine the coach running to your house every day, shaking you awake for morning training and practice? What would you say? 'I'm too tired to show up for the game today?' And yet these are the guys you most admire!"

A patient came in and brought her mother and aunt, asking if it was okay for them to stay for her session. To that I responded, "Of course, we're just one big happy family!"

One woman who was afraid to talk about her sexual fantasies opened up when I joked, "Well, it's just between us girls."

Communication Suggestions for Therapists

What follows are some general guidelines for communicating with a border-line. We as therapists need to keep in mind three things: (1) how to enlist the help of the borderline to maximize therapy, (2) how to bond with the part of the borderline that is vulnerable, and (3) how to most effectively prime the borderline for necessary confrontation, taking into consideration timing and preparation.

- Empathize with the vulnerability and the pain, not with the aggression. Do not be afraid to confront the aggression. Speak directly to the aggression with technical neutrality.
  - You are not allowed to hit your wife, but I can certainly understand how she stirs up things in you that make you enraged.
- Always let the borderline be aware that with therapy he is not just giving, that he will also get something in return.
  - Your commitment to therapy will, in the long run, make you feel less anxious, happier, and more productive. You will be doing something for yourself that no amount of success in business or the arts can offer.
- Always remind the borderline that we are engaging in a conversation, not a monologue.
- Listen to the words. Stay with the thematic material, making use of the patient's words.
- Avoid such advice as, "If you have a headache, then take an aspirin. If you can't sleep, then take a sleeping pill." Although the advice makes sense and is useful, it also typically makes borderlines feel abandoned. Therapists are often frustrated when patients do not take heed to good advise because they fail to understand that borderlines are more concerned with bonding with the pain than healing.
- Bond with some aspect of the borderline that has relevance and importance.
  - You think emotions and feelings are bad, but in order to act and perform, you need to get connected to your feelings and emotions.
- Help patients get in contact with their internal objects (betraying, rejecting, abusive).
  - Of course, there are always people who can betray us, but the worst betrayer is the internal betrayer within yourself, persecuting you,

putting yourself down, and chastising yourself "for everything you do" (critical superego).

- Try to wean the borderline away from feelings to needs. Feelings are often fallacious.
  - An obsessive–compulsive disorder (OCD) borderline husband fears that, if he gives way to his wife's demands, he will be weak and powerless: "After her screaming and histrionic outburst, I decided not to go out for Father's Day. I don't want my wife to think I am a slave to her demands." The therapist might reply, "Listen to what is needed, not to the aggression. We go out for Father's Day because it is a family event."
- Set the stage. Prepare the borderline for confrontation.
  - I know what I am about to say may stir up an old feelings that you are being used. But when I bring up a past-due bill, please be reassured that this is not about using you, but more about taking care of my needs. I know you are busy and preoccupied with your new job and many other important things. But I do need to bring this to your attention. (As opposed to saying, "You neglected to pay your bill on time for the past six months.")
- Be direct. Tell the borderline what you need in terms of treatment commitment, and do not play into the borderline's victimization or seduction.
- Continually remind the borderline why he/she sought treatment in the first place. Set goals, reevaluate, and remind patients of the treatment goals.
- Avoid asking too many questions and obtaining lengthy histories, which will make the borderline impatient. Instead, mirror and contain. The history and background information will automatically unfold within the context of the therapeutic experience and the transference.
- Avoid self-disclosure. The borderline may lure the therapist into sharing his/her personal life.
- Listen and be attentive. Maintain good eye contact, speak with meaning and conviction. Speak directly to the issues.
- Use short, clear sentences; keep responses direct; mirror and reflect sentiments with simple responses and few questions.
- When lost, keep in mind how you might respond to a "normal" person.
- Repeatedly talk to the borderline about the importance of healthy dependency needs as opposed to parasitic ones (bonding through pain, illness, and victimization).

- Remind the borderline how he/she tends to shame/blame/attack whenever personally injured.
- Try to pinpoint the exact area of anxiety (the V-spot).
- Remember that timing and preparation are necessary for effective communication.

Repetitive Themes: Listen to the Words

The therapist who listens to the words has an opportunity to transform something scary, frightening, or even disgusting into something meaningful that is more suitable for thinking—or what Bion refers to as detoxification. A patient with a severe borderline personality disorder and narcissistic characteristics invariably starts every session with "I'm so pissed. I feel like shit, and everyone treats me like shit. Everyone around me is an asshole."

> *So you are telling us that your feelings are shit and piss and that they belong in an asshole. In reality, you are referring to the feelings you are afraid to acknowledge, which are your treasures, and far from piss and shit. Feelings don't belong in an asshole or a toilet; rather, they are to be expressed. But I understand why you think that way because when you were little your mother made you feel as though you were worthless, that you were not a valuable little baby but a piece of shit.*

To this the patient replies, "Don't tell me about my treasures! I'm telling you I feel like piss and shit!" To this the therapist replies,

> *But your feelings are fallacious, and they are not really feelings; they are just words you are evacuating to get rid of a part of you that feels anxious and shameful. You think they are feelings because they come from your gut, but in essence they are your defenses.*

The following are examples of how the therapist can use the patient's words to analyze and detoxify the problem.

Emotional Bankruptcy

A couple was about to go into foreclosure when they came into treatment. Both were very angry and blamed one another for the potential loss of their home. They were clearly in Phase One of blame/shame and attack. The therapist let them know she could not help them with the "real" bankruptcy, but could help with the emotional one. The therapist also cautioned the couple that if they kept blaming/shaming and attacking each other they would both end up empty and overdrawn on their emotional resources. This emotional bankruptcy can be even worse than a financial one.

A Weighty Problem

A borderline patient who is a model was concerned that for the last few years she had been unable to lose weight. She unleashed a barrage of complaints and conflicts. To this the therapist said, "Of course, there is a real 'weight' in pounds, but what you are talking about is emotional weight. You are carrying some very heavy baggage that you brought here with you. So before we do anything we have to lighten you up emotionally." The patient felt relief when she realized that her bodily weight issue masked the "real" emotional weight—an archaic injury that weighed heavily on her heart. In this case, the truth was revealed to her, but in such a way that it was empathic and transforming.

General Suggestions for Therapists

- Use the language of dialectics to show the two faces of the borderline.
    - A patient who has internalized and identified with a scary father communicates in harsh, aggressive tones and resists the therapist's attempt to teach her empathy and better communication skills. "That doesn't sound right to me; it sounds phony." To this the therapist responds, "Why, this way of communicating should be less phony than the aggressive, internalized voice of your father, which is certainly not you."
- Help your borderline patient gradually get in contact with his/her internal objects.
    - An OCD borderline husband drives his wife crazy because all he does is clean and file. If there is any dirt, laundry or garbage in the house, he attacks his wife, making her feel like the "dirty" one. To this the therapist might reply. "Yes he can make you feel like you are the dirty one and he is squeaky clean, but we must also see how there is an internal part of you, some leftover baggage from the past, that identifies with the dirt."

- Bond with something important in the borderline's world by persuading the borderline that, rather than attacking their objects, they can confront and ask for what they need.
  - The therapist can advise, "I think you are confusing a confrontation with abuse and mistreatment. Confrontation is merely clarifying and telling someone what you need. What you call demanding and nagging, I call having normal and healthy needs!"
- Be sure to help the borderline patient learn to be cautious about identifying with and internalizing the negative thoughts and projections of others.
  - My husband goes into bouts of silence. He refuses to talk to me, does not answer my questions, and then suddenly he has an outburst of rage. I feel so terrible when he does this. It reminds me of my father, who would never answer my questions and made me feel as though I do not exist. Then I start to attack my husband back, and this is when I lose it.

In this case, the therapist must carefully help the patient disidentify and not take in the painful projections. Point out to the patient that her husband's silence has nothing to do with her being a bad person. She needs to be told that she does indeed exist but that when she internalizes her husband's negativity she begins to feel like a nothing. This occurs when the old baggage from the past (the V-spot) gets carried into her current relationship. To this the therapist must reply, "Tell your husband he need not remain silent, that you will not attack him, and whatever he says you will do your best to understand his feelings (unlike his father who would beat him). Also, let your husband know that if he doesn't share his feelings and remains silent he will end up exploding like a pressure cooker, because no one can hold such feelings inside for any length of time."

- Avoid attacking and critical remarks. Start a conversation by asking the borderline questions like "How was your day? How are you feeling? What happened at the audition?" Then gradually and gently let the borderline know that you do not mean to take the focus off him/her, but that you would like to talk about something he/she said that was hurtful. "May I have your permission to talk about—?"

- Sometimes it is best to say nothing, to avoid being needy or demanding, and to wait until the borderline feels like talking. Since needs and wants make the borderline feel vulnerable and dependent, a state they cannot tolerate, they project their needs onto others, transforming them into the "needy" ones. Waiting can be frustrating but often beneficial. Eventually the borderline will have to ask for something and will start the process of communication.
- Listen carefully to the words of the borderline patient, then use and recycle them to give meaning and purpose to your dialogue.

General Suggestions for Teachers/Students/Artists

The suggestions made in this chapter are certainly applicable to teachers, students, and artists. Teachers must always present a positive outlook when critiquing a student's work, while at the same time acting as a mirroring object for them. "I love your composition. I think it shows a great deal of creativity and potential for more thoughts on this subject. I would, however, suggest that you cut out a few extra paragraphs because they are unnecessary and detract from your major points."

As an elementary school teacher, I noticed there were special qualities in certain very creative children. They refused to conform to the classroom standards and often were punished because their behavior was judged unacceptable. Teachers frequently failed to recognize that many of these children had intense creative and artistic passions and were extremely frustrated because no one would help guide them. One fifth grade child, Bobby, refused to do his math and other homework assignments. Instead of paying attention in class he was distracted, and when asked to participate was withdrawn and inattentive. Meanwhile, a very creative and astute teacher noticed that he was always drawing cartoons. Pages of his notebooks were devoted to one cartoon after another. When she scheduled a teacher/parent conference, she found Bobby's mother frustrated and angry with her son's "waste of time drawing those stupid cartoons." The teacher decided to post the cartoons on the bulletin boards at the school's entrance. Eventually, the child started to receive prizes and recognition for his artwork, and the teacher formed a healthy and creative bond with Bobby.

Closing Thoughts

Communication with a borderline is most certainly not simple. My intention in this volume has been to encourage therapists, partners, and colleagues of borderline personalities to find a new and innovative approach to communicating effectively with a borderline. In addition, this book encourages all who interact with borderlines to be aware of how they often distort and misinterpret your words, hearing them in a much different way than you meant them. The unique language of "dialectics" is intended to address the split parts (the beaten-down child and the seductively aggressive adult) of the borderline personality, giving equal attention to the two sides so that integration and a cohesive self can result. Therapists must consistently be aware of this split, and how borderlines defend against normal, healthy states of vulnerability and dependency by becoming bullies, seducers, sociopaths, and other forms of perpetrators.

So, as the curtain closes on the borderline drama, let me say that I hope this book has revealed a new perspective on engaging in meaningful dialogue with the borderlines you treat or love or deal with in your work. My aim has been to foster greater understanding of what it takes to open up crucial channels of communication with a borderline and keep them flowing freely. This book has been written with great respect for the cast of characters involved and with much hope that it will promote heightened awareness of the need for sensitive, thoughtful communication that leads to healthy, intimate, loving, meaningful, lasting relationships.

Appendix

Description	*Traits*	*Example*
The Borderline: General Overview	Borderlines suffer from privation and deprivation, delusions, and distortions. Their internal conflicts center primarily on shame, blame, attacking defenses, attachment, and bonding issues. Their inability to deal with mourning and loss, or to face internal defeats, as well as their tendency to project unwanted parts of themselves onto others keeps them in an endless state of impoverishment. Even though they may be perpetrators, they form parasitic bonds with others and view themselves as victims.	You do not need to get sick, threaten suicide, or have car accidents to let me know you have needs.
Pathological Borderline	Pathological borderlines can be described as the least toxic type of borderline for they are not generally physically abusive or outwardly sadistic. However, they are manipulative, overdependent, clingy, and will do anything to bond with their objects through pain and victimization. They have a cult-like mentality, are dominated by such primitive defenses as shame, splitting, projection, and envy. They want to dominate and tend to consume and take over their love relations. They also have histrionic and bipolar aspects.	No wonder you feel so empty. As soon as you get a thought you get rid of it and believe that others know more than you. So basically you are the one who is abandoning you.
Malignant Borderline	Malignant borderlines are similar to malignant narcissists but with extreme paranoid and antisocial features. They are basically evil, with no sense of conscience or morality and, under the guise of "the cause," will act out their most heinous fantasies. The need to retaliate and revenge becomes more pervasive than life itself. "We crashed into the buildings on 9/11 because we were on a mission!"	Because you cannot allow yourself to feel sad and deal with losses, you must now seek revenge against those who you feel caused the damage.

(*Continued*)

Summary: Eight Types of Borderlines (CONTINUED)

Description	Traits	Example
Depressive Borderline	Depressive borderlines approximate a reverse narcissist. They are so depleted of narcissistic supplies from the external environment that they turn inward in a form of self-hatred. The depressive borderline sinks into a state of morbidity, dominated by a very strong critical and punitive superego. They often confuse normal states of mourning and loss with depression.	I do not think you are depressed. Because you cannot tolerate feeling vulnerable, you have not mourned your losses and are confusing depression with loss.
Obsessive– Compulsive Borderline	The obsessive–compulsive has a more developed and well-integrated ego, a better tolerance for anxiety and impulse control, as well as a harshly strict but well-integrated superego. At the lower spectrum of functioning, obsessive–compulsives are obsessed with orderliness, cleanliness, and perfectionism. They are devoid of feelings, are workaholics, and invariably put their partners down for having emotional needs or desires. They keep their partners on hold and never have enough time for them. Because obsessive–compulsives confuse needs and desires with dirt and disgust, they will find justification to work constantly under the guise of efficiency or the "good cause." They will also do anything to avoid intimacy.	You have married a woman who is the opposite of you, a histrionic. Although you find her overly emotional, she represents parts of yourself long ago abandoned, and so you confuse neediness with mess and dirt.
Antisocial Borderline	The antisocial borderline presents a serious superego defect and can be described as lacking the capacity for empathy, remorse, or guilt for their wrongdoings. They mirror the narcissist in that they both display a grandiose self and exaggerated sense of entitlement; however, antisocial borderlines are more destructive than narcissists in that they exploit and devalue others, lie, steal, embezzle. The only way to talk to an antisocial is to address the fear of being caught.	You do not really feel remorse. You feel sad because you got caught!

	Summary: Eight Types of Borderlines (CONTINUED)	
Description	*Traits*	*Example*
Passive–Aggressive Borderline	Although the passive–aggressive personality type no longer exists as a separate category, I have resurrected it for the purposes of couple therapy. These are the couch-potato husbands and the forgetful wives. "I'll do it later; I'll do it tomorrow. I was going to do it today, but the car broke down." They forget, delay, avoid, cajole, make an endless barrage of excuses—in short, do anything to protect the good little child from the screaming mommy. The passive–aggressive's primary aim is to coerce (unconsciously) a partner to behave in a certain way to recreate the parent–child dyad.	It is good that you got angry. This is better than to set up others to express your anger for you.
Histrionic Borderline	Histrionic borderlines cry easily, have excessive parasitic dependency needs, and display their emotions on their sleeves. In some instances, histrionic borderlines may appear very narcissistic but use their seductive powers to bond provocatively with their objects.	There is no need to yell, cry, or scream to be heard here. I do not need drama to hear how important it is for you to get your needs met.
Cultural Borderline	The cultural borderline will do anything to hold onto a nationalistic pride that encompasses his/her own country's values and will resist vehemently adapting to the customs of another country. On a global level some will rebel/retaliate or, at the extreme level, become freedom fighters, terrorists, suicide bombers. The cultural borderline's cult-like mentality encourages him to do anything to maintain the group's cohesion or collective identity. One must deal not only with the cultural borderline himself but also with the array of cultural traditions and ideologies he espouses.	You say in your country people are generous and giving and very hospitable, and yet when it comes to giving to your wife, you are withholding. That seems to go against your culture (finding the cross-cultural hook).

Glossary

Attunement: Attunement is the rhythm of the heart and soul as it blends with another person. According to Winnicott (1965), it is the mother/infant experience of togetherness, that beautiful moment of closeness against the backdrop of dialectic tensions involving the dread of separateness. It is that special moment when the infant and mommy are one—in total harmony, bliss, and synchronicity. Whether it be the dancer and the pianist, the musician and the conductor, the painter and his canvas, or the patient with the analyst, I refer to two types of attunement: (1) the moment of togetherness and (2) sensing the rhythm and timing of the other.

Borderline personality: This personality disorder designates a defect in the maternal attachment bond as an overconcern with the "other." Many have affixed the term "as-if personalities" to borderlines. This refers to their tendency to subjugate or compromise themselves. They question their sense of existence, suffer from acute abandonment and persecutory anxiety, and tend to merge with others in very painful ways in order to achieve a sense of bonding. Under close scrutiny and stress, they distort, misperceive, have poor impulse control, and turn suddenly against self and others (to attack, blame, find fault, and get even).

Containment: A term employed by Wilfred Bion, containment describes the interaction between the mother and the infant. Bion believed that all psychological barriers universally dissolve when the mind acts as receiver of communicative content, which the mother does in a state of reverie by using her own alpha function. Containment connotes the capacity for transformation of the data of emotional experience into meaningful feelings and thoughts. The mother's capacity to withstand the child's anger, frustrations, and intolerable feelings becomes the container for these effects. This can occur if the mother is able to sustain intolerable behaviors long enough to decode or detoxify painful feelings into a more digestible form.

Couple transference: *Couple transference* is a term I devised to describe what happens during treatment when the partners jointly project onto the therapist some unconscious fantasy—for example, making the therapist feel guilty for stopping the session on time, giving them a bill, not changing appointment times, etc. Together the partners form a *folie à deux*.

Cultural V-spot: The cultural V-spot is a collectively shared archaic experience from the mythological or historical past that evokes painful thoughts and memories for the group (e.g., burning of the temple, loss of land to Israel, the expulsion of Ishmael to the desert with his abandoned mother, Hagar).

Depressive position: This is a term devised by Melanie Klein to describe a state of mourning and sadness in which integration and reparation take place. In this state not everything is seen in terms of black and white. There is more tolerance, guilt, remorse, self-doubt, frustration, pain, and confusion. One is more responsible for one's action. There is the realization not of what things should be, but of the way they are. As verbal expression increases, one may feel sadness, but one may also feel a newly regained sense of aliveness.

Dual projective identification: Whereas projective identification is a one-way process, dual projective identification is a two-way process that lends itself to conjoint treatment. One partner projects a negative feeling onto the other, who then identifies or overidentifies with the negativity being projected. "I'm not stupid! Don't call me stupid!"

Ego: The ego is part of an intrapsychic system responsible for functioning (thinking, reality testing, judgment). It is the mediator between the id and superego. The function of the ego is to observe the external world, preserving a true picture by eliminating old memory traces left by early impressions and perceptions.

Empathology: Empathology is a new language I devised for talking to the eight different types of narcissists I delineated and the various communication styles applicable to each type. It is a term I abstracted from Heinz Kohut's concept of empathy. Empathology is an essential therapeutic technique in treating the narcissistic personality disorder.

Envy: Klein made a distinction between envy and jealousy. Envy is a part-object function and is not based on love. She considers envy to be the most primitive and fundamental emotion. It exhausts external objects, and is destructive in nature. Envy is possessive, controlling, and does not allow in outsiders.

***Folie à deux*:** In general terms, *folie à deux* refers to Melanie Klein's notion of projective identification, whereby two people project their delusional fantasies back and forth and engage in a foolish "dance." The partners are wrapped up in a shared delusional fantasy, and each engages in and believes in the outrageous scheme of the other. Usually the term applies to both oppositional and collusive couples. In some cases there is triangulation, which is a three-part relationship in which two people form a covert or overt bond against another member.

Guilt: Guilt is a higher form of development than shame. Guilt has an internal punishing voice that operates at the level of the superego (an internalized, punitive, harsh parental figure). There are two kinds of guilt: valid guilt and invalid guilt. Valid guilt occurs when the person should feel guilty. Invalid guilt comes from a punitive and persecutory superego.

Internal objects: Internal objects result from an intrapsychic process whereby unconscious fantasies that are felt to be persecutory, threatening, or dangerous are denounced, split off, and projected. Internal objects emanate from the part of the ego that has been introjected. Klein believed that the infant internalizes good "objects" or the "good breast." However, if the infant perceives the world as bad and dangerous, the infant internalizes the "bad breast."

Jealousy: Jealousy, a higher form of development than envy, is a whole-object relationship whereby one desires the object but does not seek to destroy it or the oedipal rival (father and siblings, those who take mother away). Jealousy, unlike envy, is a triangular relationship based on love, wherein one desires to be part of or included in the group, family, clan, nation.

Manic defenses: The experience of excitement (mania) offsets feelings of despair, loss, anxiety, and vulnerability. Manic defenses evolve as a defense against depressive anxiety, guilt, and loss. They are based on omnipotent denial of psychic reality and on object relations characterized by a massive degree of triumph, control, and hostility. Some manic defenses work in the ego.

Mirroring: This is a term devised by Heinz Kohut that describes the "gleam" in a mother's eye, which mirrors the child's exhibitionistic display. This maternal response to the child's narcissistic–exhibitionist displays confirm the child's self-esteem. Eventually these responses are channeled into more realistic aims.

Narcissist (the *artist*): The healthy artist displays a certain amount of grandiosity, pomposity, self-involvement, self-absorption, preoccupation with self, and an obsessive investment in perfectionism. However, this does not interfere with the artist's creative process or ability to have healthy object relations ("aesthetic survival"). The pathological artist is the one who functions at the extreme end of pathological narcissism and is dominated by such defenses as envy, control, competition, domination, where winning becomes more pervasive that the joy of the creative process.

Narcissistic/borderline relationship: These two personality types enter into a psychological "dance" and consciously or unconsciously stir up highly charged feelings that fulfill early unresolved conflicts in each other. The revelation is that each partner needs the other to play out his or her own personal relational drama. Those who engage in these beleaguered relationships are developmentally arrested people who bring into their current relationships archaic experiences embedded in old sentiments.

Narcissistic personality: These individuals are dominated by omnipotence, grandiosity, and exhibitionist features. They become strongly invested in others and experience them as self-objects. In order to preserve this "special" relationship with their self-objects (others), they tend to withdraw or isolate themselves by concentrating on perfection and power.

Object relations: Object relations is a powerful theory of unconscious internal object relations in a dynamic interplay with current interpersonal experience. It examines unconscious fantasies and motivations, reflecting how a person can distort reality by projecting and identifying with bad objects. This approach to understanding intrapsychic and internal conflict—including the patients, projections, introjections, fantasies, and distortion, delusions, and split-off aspects of the self—is based on how one relates and interacts with others in the external world. Klein developed the idea of pathological splitting of "good" and "bad" objects through the defensive process of projection and introjection in relation to primitive anxiety and the death instinct (based on biology).

Paranoid–schizoid position: The paranoid–schizoid position is a fragmented position in which thoughts and feelings are split off and projected because the psyche cannot tolerate feelings of pain, emptiness, loneliness, rejection, humiliation, or ambiguity. Klein viewed this position as the earliest phase of development, part-object functioning, and the beginning of the primitive superego (undeveloped). If the child views mother as a "good breast," the child will maintain good, warm, and hopeful feelings about the environment. If, on the other hand, the infant experiences mother as a "bad breast," the child is more likely to experience the environment as bad, attacking, and persecutory. Klein, more than any of her followers, understood the primary importance of the need for mother and the breast.

Part objects: The first relational unit is the feeding experience with the mother and the infant's relation to the breast. Klein believed the breast is the child's first possession. However, because it is so desired it also becomes the source of the infant's envy, greed, and hatred and is therefore susceptible to the infant's fantasized attacks. The infant internalizes the mother as good or bad or, to be more specific, as a "part object" (a "good breast" or "bad breast"). As the breast is felt to contain a great part of the infant's death instinct (persecutory anxiety), it simultaneously establishes libidinal forces, giving way to the baby's first ambivalence. One part of the mother is loved and idealized, while the other is destroyed by the infant's oral, anal, sadistic, or aggressive impulses. In clinical terms Klein referred to this as pathological splitting. Here a parent is seen as a *function* for what that the parent can provide (e.g., in infancy the breast, in later life money, material objects, etc.). "I only love women who have big breasts!"

Persecutory anxiety: This is the part of the psyche that threatens and terrifies the patient. It relates to what Klein has referred to as the primitive superego, an undifferentiated state that continually warns the patient of imminent danger (often unfounded). Paranoid anxiety is a feature associated with the death instinct and is more persecutory in nature. It implies the kind of anxiety from the primitive superego that is more explosive and volatile than that from the more developed superego.

Projective identification: This is a process whereby one splits off an unwanted aspect of the self and puts it into the object, which identifies or overidentifies with that which is being projected. In other words, the self experiences the unconscious defensive mechanism and translocates itself into the other. Under the influence of projective identification, one becomes vulnerable to the coercion, manipulation, or control of the person doing the projecting.

Psychohistory: Psychohistory does for the group what psychoanalysis does for the individual. It offers a broader perspective from which to view cross-cultural differences. Using psychoanalytic tools and concepts, psychohistory allows a better understanding of individuals, nations, governments, and political events—very much as a therapist analyzes the couple as a symbolic representation of a political group or nation (deMause 2002a, 2002b, 2006).

Reparation: The desire for the ego to restore an injured love object by coming to terms with one's own guilt and ambivalence. The process of reparation begins in the depressive position and starts when one develops the capacity to mourn, as well as tolerate and contain the feelings of loss and guilt.

Schizoid personality: The central features of the schizoid are their defenses of attachment, aloofness, and indifference to others. The schizoid, although difficult to treat, is usually motivated, unlike the passive–aggressive. However, because of his detachment and aloofness, the schizoid personality lacks the capacity to achieve social and sexual gratification. A close relationship invites the danger of being overwhelmed or suffocated, for intimacy may be envisioned as a relinquishing of independence. The schizoid differs from the obsessive–compulsive personality in that the obsessive–compulsive feels great discomfort with emotions, whereas the schizoid is lacking in the capacity to feel the emotion but at least recognizes the need. Schizoids differ from the narcissist in that they are self-sufficient and self-contained. They do not experience or suffer the same feelings of loss that borderlines and narcissists do. "Who, me? I don't care, I have my work, my computer, etc.!"

Self objects: This is a term devised by Heinz Kohut. A forerunner of self psychology, the term refers to an interpersonal process whereby the analyst provides basic functions for the patient. These functions are used to make up for failures in the past by caretakers who were lacking in mirroring, empathic attunement, and had faulty responses to their children. Kohut reminds us that psychological disturbances are caused by failures from idealized objects, and that, for the rest of their lives, patients may need self objects that provide good mirroring responses.

Self psychology: Heinz Kohut revolutionized analytic thinking when he introduced a new psychology of the self that stresses the patient's subjective experience. Unlike with object relations, the patient's "reality" is not considered a distortion or a projection, but rather the patient's truth. It is the patient's experience that is considered of utmost importance. Self psychology, with its emphasis on the empathic mode, implies that the narcissistic personality is more susceptible to classical interpretations. Recognition of splitting and projection is virtually nonexistent among self psychologists.

Shame: Shame is a matter between the person and his group or society, while guilt is primarily a matter between a person and his conscious. Shame is the defense against the humiliation of having needs that are felt to be dangerous and persecutory. Shame is associated with anticipatory anxiety and annihilation fantasies. "If I tell my boyfriend what I really need, he will abandon me!"

Single and dual projective identification (*as it pertains to conjoint treatment*): In single projective identification, one takes in the other person's projections by identifying with that which is being projected. Dual projective identification is a term I devised to describe how both partners take in the projections of the other and identify or overidentify with that which is being projected (the splitting of the ego). Thus, one may project guilt while the other projects shame. "You should be ashamed of yourself for being so needy! When you're so needy, I feel guilty!"

Splitting: Splitting occurs when a person cannot keep two contradictory thoughts or feelings in mind at the same time and therefore keeps the conflicting feelings apart, focusing on just one of them.

Superego: The literature refers to different kinds of superegos. Freud's superego concerns itself with moral judgment, what people think. It depicts an introjected whole figure, a parental voice or image that operates from a point of view of morality, telling the child how to follow the rules and what happens if they do not. The superego deals with the "dos, don'ts, oughts, and shoulds" and represents the child's compliance and conformity with strong parental figures. Freud's superego is the internalized image that continues to live inside the child, controlling or punishing. Klein's superego centers on the shame and humiliation of having needs, thoughts, and feelings that are felt to be more persecutory and hostile in nature and invade the psyche as an unmentalized experience.

V-spot: The *V-spot* is a term I devised to describe the most sensitive area of emotional vulnerability that gets aroused when one partner hits an emotional raw spot in the object. It is the emotional counterpart to the physical "G-spot." The V-spot is the heart of our most fragile area at emotional sensitivity, known in the literature as the archaic injury, a product of early trauma that one holds onto. With arousal of the V-spot comes the loss of sense and sensibility; everything shakes and shifts like an earthquake (memory, perception, judgment, reality).

Whole objects: The beginning of the depressive position is marked by the infant's awareness of his mother as a "whole object." As the infant matures and as verbal expression increases, the infant achieves more cognitive ability and acquires the capacity to love the mother as a separate person with separate needs, feelings, and desires. In the depressive position, guilt and jealousy become the replacement for shame and envy. Ambivalence and guilt are experienced and tolerated in relation to whole objects. One no longer seeks to destroy the objects or the oedipal rival (father and siblings, who take mother away), but can begin to live amicably with them.

Withdrawal versus detachment: Detachment should not be confused with withdrawal. Withdrawal is actually a healthier state because it maintains a certain libidinal attachment to the object. When one detaches, one splits off and goes into a state of despondency. Children who are left alone, ignored, or neglected for long periods of time enter into a phase of despair (Bowlby). The child's active protest for the missing or absent mother gradually diminishes, and the child no longer makes demands. When this occurs, the infant goes into detachment mode or pathological mourning. Apathy, lethargy, and listlessness become the replacement for feelings (anger, rage, betrayal, abandonment).

Bibliography

American Psychiatric Association. (1994). *Diagnostic and Statistical Manual of Mental Disorders*, 4th ed. Washington, DC.

Berton, P. (1995, November). Understanding Japanese negotiating behavior. *ISOP Intercom* (Los Angeles: UCLA), 18(2), 1–8.

Berton, P. (2001). *Japan on the psychologist's couch*. Los Angeles: University of Southern California, Emerti Center.

Bienenfeld, F. (1986). *Child custody medication*. Palo Alto, CA: U.S. Science and Behavior Books.

Bion, W. R. (1961). *Experiences in groups and other papers*. London: Tavistock.

Bion, W. R. (1962). *Learning from experience*. London: Heinemann.

Bion, W. R. (1967). *Second thoughts. Selected papers on psycho-analysis*. New York: Jason Aronson.

Bion, W. R. (1977). *Seven servants. Four works by Wilfred R. Bion*. New York: Jason Aronson.

Bowlby, J. (1969). *Attachment and loss* (3 vols.). New York: Basic Books.

CAMFT (2002, March/April). The psychological make-up of a suicide bomber. *The California Therapist*, 14.

Carlson, J., & Sperry, L. (Eds.). (1998). *The disordered couple*. New York: Brunner/Mazel.

Cullen, D. (2009). *Columbine*. Hachette Book Group: New York.

deMause, L. (2002a). *The emotional life of nations*. New York: Karnac Books.

deMause, L. (2002b). The childhood origins of terrorism. *Journal of Psychohistory*, 29, 340–349.

deMause, L. (2006). The childhood origins of the holocaust. *Journal of Psychohistory*, 33, 204.

deMause, L. (2007). The killer mutterland. *Journal of Psychohistory*, 34, 278–300.

Dicks, H. (1967). *Marital tensions. Clinical studies toward a psychological theory of interaction*. New York: Basic Books.

Doi, T. (1973). *The anatomy of dependence*. Tokyo: Kodansha International.

Dutton, D., & Painter, S. L. (1981). Traumatic bonding. The development of emotional attachments in battered women and other relationships of intermittent abuse. *Victimology. An International Journal*, 6, 139–155.

Endleman, R. (1989). *Love and sex in twelve cultures*. New York: Psychic Press.

Fairbairn, W. R. D. (1940). Schizoid factors in the personality. In *Psychoanalytic studies of the personality* (pp. 3–27). London: Routledge & Kegan

Freud, S. (1905). Freud quoted in *The first dream fragment of an analysis of a case of hysteria*. Cited in Wikipedia—http://en.wikiquote.org/wiki/Sigmund_Freud.

Freud, S. (1908). Creative writers and day-dreaming In J. Strachey (Ed. & Trans.), *The standard edition of the complete works of Sigmund Freud* (Vol. IX, pp. 141–153). London: Hogarth Press.

Freud, S. (1909/1955). Notes upon a case of obsessional neurosis. In J. Strachey (Ed. & Trans.), *The standard edition of the complete works of Sigmund Freud* (Vol. 10, pp. 153–318). London: Hogarth Press.

Freud, S. (1918). From the history of an infantile neurosis. In J. Strachey (Ed. & Trans.), *The standard edition of the complete works of Sigmund Freud.* (Vol. 14, pp. 1–122). London: Hogarth Press.

Freud, S. (1914/1957). On narcissism: An introduction. In J. Strachey (Ed. & Trans.), *The standard edition of the complete works of Sigmund Freud.* (Vol. 14, pp. 69–102). London: Hogarth Press.

Freud, S. (1920/1955). *Beyond the pleasure principle.* London: Hogarth Press.

Freud, S. (1921/1979). Group psychology and the analysis of the ego. In J. Strachey (Ed. & Trans.), *The standard edition of the complete works of Sigmund Freud* (Vol. 18, pp. 65–143). London: Hogarth Press.

Freud, S. (1923). *The ego and id.* New York: Norton.

Fruggetti, A. (2006). *The high conflict couple: A dialectic behavior therapy guide to finding peace, intimacy, and validation.* Oakland, CA: New Harbinger Publisher.

Gay, P. (1988). *Freud. A life for our times.* New York: Norton.

Giovacchini, P. (1993). *Borderline patients, the psychosomatic focus and the therapeutic process.* Northvale, NJ: Jason Aronson.

Grotstein, J. (1981). *Splitting and projective identification.* New York: Jason Aronson.

Grotstein, J. (1987). Meaning, meaningless, and the "black hole." Self and international regulation as a new paradigm for psychoanalysis and neuroscience: An introduction. Unpublished manuscript.

Grotstein, J. (1993). Boundary difficulties in borderline patients. In L. B. Boyer & P. Giovacchini (Eds.), *Master clinicians: On treating the regressed patient* (pp. 107–142). Northvale, NJ, and London: Jason Aronson.

Gunderson, J. G. (1984). *Borderline personality disorder.* Washington, DC: American Psychiatric Press.

Imai, M. (1981). 16 ways to avoid saying no. *The Nihon Keizai Shimbun (Japan Economic Journal),* Japan.

Isay, J. (2008). *Walking on eggshells: Navigating the delicate relationship between adult children and parents.* New York: Doubleday/Flying Dolphin Press.

Johnson, F. (1993). *Dependency and Japanese socialization: Psychoanalytic and anthropological investigations into Amae.* New York: New York University Press.

Kernberg, O. (1975). *Borderline conditions and pathological narcissism.* New York: Jason Aronson.

Kernberg, O. (1985a). *Borderline conditions and pathological narcissism.* New York: Jason Aronson.

Kernberg, O. (1985b). *Internal world and external reality: Object relations theory applied.* New York: Jason Aronson.

Kernberg, O. (1992). *Aggression in personality disorders and perversions.* New Haven, CT: Yale University Press.

Kernberg, O. (1991). Sadomasochism, sexual excitement, and perversion. *Journal of the American Psychoanalytic Association, 39,* 333–362.

Kernberg, O. (1995). *Love relations: Normality and pathology.* New Haven, CT, and London: New Haven Press.

Klein, M. (1927). Criminal tendencies in normal children. *International Journal of Psychoanalysis, 42,* 4–8.

Klein, M. (1948). Mourning and its relation to manic states. In *Contributions to psycho-analysis. 1921–1945.* London: Hogarth Press. (Original work published in 1921.)

Klein, M. (1957). *Envy and gratitude.* New York: Basic Books.

Klein, M. (1975). Love, guilt, and reparation. In R. E. Money-Kryle (Ed.), *The writings of Melanie Klein, Vol. I—Love, guilt and reparation and other works 1921–1945* (pp. 306–343). New York: The Free Press. (Original work published 1937.)

Klein, M. (1984). Narrative of a child analysis. In R. E. Money-Kryle (Ed.), *The writings of Melanie Klein* (Vol. 4). New York: Free Press. (Original work published in 1961.)

Kobrin, N. (2010). *The banality of suicide terrorism: The naked truth about the psychology of Islamic suicide bombings.* Dulles, VA: Potomac Books.

Kobrin, N. (2010). Personal communication.

Kobrin, N., & Lachkar, J. (2005). The she bomber. Symposium, September 9, 2005, http://www.frontpagemag.com.

Kohut, H. (1971). *The analysis of the self.* New York: International Universities Press.

Kohut, H. (1977). *The restoration of the self.* New York: International Universities Press.

Lachkar, J. (1986). Narcissistic/borderline couples: Implications for mediation. Courts beware of the borderline. *Conciliation Court Review,* 24(1), 31–43.

Lachkar, J. (1992). *The narcissistic/borderline couple: A psychoanalytic perspective to marital conflict.* New York: Brunner/Mazel.

Lachkar, J. (1993a). Paradox of peace: *Folie à deux* in marital and political relationships. *Journal of Psychohistory,* 20(3), 275–287.

Lachkar, J. (1993b). Political and marital conflict. *Journal of Psychohistory,* 22(2), 199–211.

Lachkar, J. (1997). Narcissistic/borderline couples: A psychodynamic approach to conjoint treatment. In J. Carlson & L. Sperry (Eds.), *The disordered couple* (pp. 259–282). New York: Brunner/Mazel.

Lachkar, J. (1998a). *The many faces of abuse: Treating the emotional abuse of high-functioning women.* Northvale, NJ: Jason Aronson.

Lachkar, J. (1998b, July). *Aggression and cruelty in cross-cultural couples.* Paper presented at the Psychohistory Congress, Paris.

Lachkar, J. (2000). Slobodan and Mirjana Milosevic: The dysfunctional couple that destroyed the Balkans. Unpublished paper.

Lachkar, J. (2001). Narcissism in dance. *Choreography and Dance: An International Journal,* 6, 23–30.

Lachkar, J. (2002). The psychological make-up of a suicide bomber. *Journal of Psychohistory,* 29(4), 349–367.

Lachkar, J. (2004a, September). Women who become undone. The many faces of abuse, review by Aimee Lee Ball. *Oprah Magazine,* pp. 300–305, 327.

Lachkar, J. (2004b). *The narcissistic/borderline couple: New approaches to marital therapy* (2nd ed.). New York: Taylor & Francis.

Lachkar, J. (2006). The psychopathology of terrorism: A cultural V-spot. *Journal of Psychohistory,* 34(2). From a paper presented at the International Psychohistorical Association, June 2005, New York University.

Lachkar, J. (2008a). *The V-spot: Healing the "V"ulnerable spot from emotional abuse.* New York: Roman and Littlefield.

Lachkar, J. (2008b). *How to talk to a narcissist.* New York: Taylor & Francis.

Lachkar, J. (2008c). Psychopathology of terrorism. Paper presented at Rand Corporation, 3rd Annual Conference: Terrorism and Global Security, May 8–9, Santa Monica, CA.

Lachkar, J. (2009). How to talk to a borderline. *The Therapist*. California Association for Marriage and Family Therapists (CAMFT), San Diego.

Lamb, H. R., Weinberger, L. E., & Gross, B. H. (1999). Community treatment of severely mentally ill offenders under the jurisdiction of the criminal justice system: A review. *Psychiatric Services*, 50(7), 907–913.

Lamb, H. R., Weinberger, L. E., & Gross, B. H. (1999). Mentally ill persons in the criminal justice system: Some perspectives. *Psychiatric Quarterly*, 75(2), 107–126.

Lansky, M. R. (1987). The borderline father: Reconstructions of young adulthood. *Psychoanalytic Inquiry*, 7, 77–98.

Lawson, C. (2002). *Understanding the borderline mother. Helping her children transcend the intense, unpredictable, and volatile relationship.* Northvale, NJ: Jason Aronson.

Linehan, M. M. (1993a). *Cognitive behavioral treatment of borderline personality disorder.* New York, London: The Guilford Press.

Linehan, M. M. (1993b). *Skills training manual for treating borderline personality disorder.* New York, London: The Guilford Press.

Loewenberg, P. (1987). *The Kristallnacht as a public degradation in ritual.* Leo Beck Institute Yearbook, 32. (Londong, Secker, & Warburg), p. 82.

Los Angeles Times. (April 17, 2006). Moussaoui has seldom acted in his best interests. A5.

Mahari, A. J. (2009). *The borderline dance and the non-borderlines' dilemma.* www.aspergeradults.ca.

Mahler, M. S., Pine, F., & Bergman, A. (1975). *The psychological birth of the human infant.* New York: Basic Books.

Martin, P., & Bird, H. M. (1959). Marriage patterns: The "lovesick" wife and the "cold sick" husband. *Psychiatry*, 22, 245–249.

Mason, P. (1998). *Stop walking on eggshells: Taking your life back when someone you care about has a borderline personality.* Oakland, CA: New Harbinger Publications.

Masterson, J. (1981). *The narcissistic and borderline disorders: An integrated developmental approach.* New York: Brunner/Mazel.

Orange County Register. (March 11, 2010). New charges will keep molester in prison, by Rachannee Sprisavasdi and Larry Welborn.

Rule, A. (2000). *The stranger beside me* (revised ed.). New American Library. New York: Penguin Putnam Inc.

Seinfeld, J. (1990). *The bad object: Handling the negative therapeutic reactions in psychotherapy.* Northvale, NJ: Jason Aronson.

Sperry, L. (2006). *Cognitive behavior therapy of SSM-IV-TR personality disorders* (2nd ed.). New York, London: Routledge, Taylor & Francis.

Sperry, L., & Maniacci, M. P. (1998). The histrionic–obsessive couple. In J. Carlson & L. Sperry (Eds.), *The Disordered Couple* (pp. 187–205). Bristol, PA: Brunner/Mazel, Inc.

The stoning of Soraya M. (2008). American drama film adapted from French–Iranian journalist Freidoune Sahebjam's 1994 book of the same name, based on a true story.

Trzepacz, P. T., & Baker, R. W. (1993). *The psychiatric mental status examination.* Oxford: Oxford University Press, p. 202.

Vaknin, S. (2007). *Personality disorders revisited.* Czech Republic: Narcissus Publications, pp. 262–264.

Winnicott, D. W. (1965). *The maturational process and the facilitating environment.* New York: International Universities Press.

Index